THE
CREATIVITY
CHALLENGE

DESIGN, EXPERIMENT, TEST, INNOVATE, BUILD, CREATE, INSPIRE, AND UNLEASH YOUR GENIUS

THE CREATIVITY CHALLENGE

TANNER CHRISTENSEN, CREATIVESOMETHING.NET

adamsmedia
Avon, Massachusetts

Published by
Adams Media, a division of F+W Media, Inc.
57 Littlefield Street, Avon, MA 02322. U.S.A.
www.adamsmedia.com

ISBN 10: 1-4405-8833-3
ISBN 13: 978-1-4405-8833-4
eISBN 10: 1-4405-8834-1
eISBN 13: 978-1-4405-8834-1

Printed in the United States of America.

10   9   8   7   6   5   4   3   2

Library of Congress Cataloging-in-Publication Data

Christensen, Tanner.
   The creativity challenge / Tanner Christensen.
      pages cm
   ISBN 978-1-4405-8833-4 (pb) -- ISBN 1-4405-8833-3 (pb) -- ISBN 978-1-4405-
8834-1 (ebook) -- ISBN 1-4405-8834-1 (ebook)
   1. Self-actualization (Psychology) 2. Creative ability. I. Title.
   BF637.S4.C49968 2015
   153.3'5--dc23
                              2015009448

Cover design by Jessica Pooler.

This book is available at quantity discounts for bulk purchases.
For information, please call 1-800-289-0963.

"Creativity can solve almost any problem. The creative act, the defeat of habit by originality, overcomes everything."

—GEORGE LOIS, AMERICAN ART DIRECTOR, DESIGNER, AND AUTHOR

INTRODUCTION

Do you ever find yourself . . .

- Unable to write that opening paragraph of your presentation?
- Wishing you could take your hobby to the next level?
- Trying to solve a difficult problem, at work or at home?
- Longing to write a book?

No matter what your age, profession, or personal interests, you need creativity in your life. Many of us want to be more creative in our lives and in our work, but it's not always easy to generate new and exciting ideas. That's because the challenge with thinking creatively is that it requires you to change how you think. More than that, creativity requires that you change how you think about thinking.

Is your brain spinning? Don't worry, that's where this book comes in. Here's a secret: You already have immense creative potential in you; you just need some help unleashing it. Within this book, you will find 150

challenges for sparking those valuable insights we so often attribute to creativity, by prompting you to think in new and unique ways.

The creative challenges involve everything from the silly (acting like a
three-year-old in order to push your boundaries), to the thoughtful (doodling with strangers in order to overcome biases in your perceptions and
gain insights from an outside perspective). Each challenge will push you
to rethink how you see the world around you in order to uncover new possibilities and ideas. By completing each challenge, you'll have a better
foundation for seeing the world in unique ways, and approaching problems
you encounter with a more creative light. You can do the challenges alone
or with a friend, once a day or all of them at once—there is no right way to
use this book.

Whether you want to be a more imaginative writer, solve problems in
your life, overcome boredom, or inspire those around you, you'll find the
creative spark you need with these exercises! Let's uncover your inner
creativity . . .

HOW TO USE THIS BOOK

You'll quickly find that this book is very easy to use. Whenever you feel stuck or uninspired, simply turn to a random page and follow the instructions to complete the creative challenge you find there. You *could* read this book in order, front to back (or back to front, if that's your thing), but you're much more likely to gain powerful insights into your thinking by picking a challenge at random. Of course, if you want to scan through all the challenges first to get a sense of the different types, you can do that too.

However, I recommend that whenever you complete a challenge you mark the page however you see fit, in order to let yourself know which challenges you've accomplished and which have yet to be explored. Bend pages, highlight passages, bookmark them, make notes, doodle over the words—whatever works for you. You'll undoubtedly get the most benefits from this book if you draw right on the pages (if you're reading from a physical copy). If you're reading the book on an electronic device, consider getting a notebook to accompany it so you can keep your doodles and writing in one place.

Another point: occasionally doing the challenges with a friend or coworker can also be beneficial. The added perspective of someone else can help make thinking differently even easier. Let the person know why you're doing the challenge, and be sure he or she is open-minded and supportive of your efforts. Doing a creative challenge is a great way to open a meeting about a difficult problem in the workplace or jump-start a book club discussion.

The Types of Creative Challenges

Before you dive headfirst into the challenges, it's important to get an understanding of the types of creative challenges within this book and how each is centered around a different mode of thinking. We'll be focusing on five specific modes and how changing any aspect of each influences your ability to think differently.

While there are certainly many more ways of thinking and problem solving than what is outlined here, these five types of processes are easy to identify, use, and categorize.

 ## Convergent

Convergent thinking requires you to combine elements of more than one idea or thing. You can think of convergent thinking like putting a puzzle together. You have to look at how different pieces can be combined to create something new. For example, do you have parts of a novel floating around in your head? These types of creative challenges will help you see if any of those parts can connect into one story line.

 ## Divergent

If convergent thinking is combining things, divergent thinking is taking them apart so you can look at their individual parts. To use divergent thinking, you bridge the gap between one thing and others by looking closely at what each has in common, no matter how small. For example, are you facing a problem getting a product manufactured? These types of challenges will help you break down the whole process into smaller parts to tackle each phase of manufacturing.

 ## Lateral

Lateral thinking is a straightforward, logical thinking process that must follow steps in order. This type of thinking requires that you follow a mode of thinking, one way or another, to end up in a new place. When you solve a math problem (like 100 + 1), you're using lateral thinking.

 ## Aesthetic

To think aesthetically is to focus on how an object or idea looks. You use aesthetic thinking when you look closely at how each part of something appears, or by imagining what would happen if one or more visual attributes of something changed. These types of challenges will help you decorate your house, put finishing touches on a painting, or design your backyard landscape.

 ## Emergent

Emergent thinking is a natural process that comes as a result of rumination. It's the most common form of creativity you may be familiar with because it's what happens when you daydream, go for a walk, or sleep. It's this type of thinking that typically results in a sudden moment that makes you want to shout "Aha!" These challenges can help you get an idea for that new ad campaign, product design, or birthday party theme.

In the pages that follow, you'll encounter each of these five methods, one after the other. When you're ready to start thinking more creatively, simply flip to a random page and let's get started.

1. PEOPLE WATCH

Research from New York University and Tel Aviv University has shown that you're more inclined to think creatively when you imagine yourself removed from a problem or situation. Imagining yourself in the mind of somebody else, for example, is a simple way to trick your brain into seeing things in new ways. The act of people watching is one way to do just that. As you watch strangers, you can imagine how they might handle a situation. That thought process allows for ideas that would otherwise be unrealistic or limited by your personal way of thinking. After all, *you* might not act a certain way, but a stranger could. Imagining how a stranger might act makes it possible for you to think of more radical and imaginative ideas than you might be used to, simply because it's not *you* acting them out, but someone else you're watching.

YOUR CHALLENGE:

Go to a public place, like a shopping center or university library, and quickly write a short story for some different people you see walking about. Combine the different traits and actions of your "characters" into one compelling story.

2. LIST 100 ALTERNATIVE USES

In 1967, a man named J.P. Guilford came up with a fun creative test called Alternative Uses. The test works like this: You think of an object—like a chair, a hat, a book, or really anything—then try to list as many possible uses as you can for that item. The alternative uses you think up allow you to see the object in an entirely new light, simply because you'll have to strain your brain to come up with a number of original ideas.

For example: this book (or the device you're reading it on) could not only be used as a book, it could be used as a hat, as a doorstop, or as a way to abruptly and painfully get someone's attention after throwing it at them (please don't do that, though).

YOUR CHALLENGE:
Come up with a list of at least 100 different uses for this book (or whatever device you're reading it on). You've already got three ideas to start!

3. WRITE ABOUT A UNIQUE SITUATION

Writing requires you to physically move your hand or fingers, using fine motor control. Writing also means that part of your brain is reading back the words as you write, using a completely different part of your brain (the visual and mental processing parts) than the motorized area. Reading as you write allows you to recapture and rethink the words as they come out onto the paper or screen.

Because of these two distinct functions, when you constrain yourself to write about a specific topic (say, a unique situation that recently occurred in your life, like catching up with an old friend or trying that new coffee place down the street), your brain approaches the task in a way no other approach allows it to: by using different parts of processing at the same time. This allows you to see the event that occurred in a more creative and imaginative way, raising themes and ideas you might originally have missed during the experience.

YOUR CHALLENGE: Write about a unique situation you recently experienced in your life. Write at least two full pages detailing the experience without worrying about grammar or perfecting what you write.

4. CHANGE ONE THING

We tend to fall into routines easily. Day in and day out, we do, say, see, and think more or less the same things repeatedly. We lose sight of how each small piece of a whole affects the outcome. One exercise you can use to break routine and see things in new ways is to change the aesthetic elements of something you encounter on a regular basis. For example, imagine what would happen if your keyboard were 1,000 times bigger, or if your hands were 1,000 times smaller.

Imagining what would happen if you changed one thing you do on a daily basis—and thinking about how that change would affect everything else—is a clever way to conquer seemingly impossible scenarios and consider how even the smallest thing you deal with impacts everything else you do.

YOUR CHALLENGE: Imagine what would happen if something in your life—your computer, your hands or eyes, your clothing, etc.—changed aesthetically (if it were much bigger, or smaller, or a different shape). Act out how you would behave if the change were real.

5. ACT LIKE YOU'RE THREE AGAIN

Three-year-olds don't have to deal with the same rules and realities adults do. Because of that, children tend to be more imaginative and creative with their ideas. They see possibilities where the rest of us see rules, boundaries, or impossibilities. That's why they're famous for writing on walls—you see a perfectly painted living room that shouldn't be touched; they see a blank canvas. Even if it's just for 30 minutes, seeing life from the angle of a semi-careless child can give you a new perspective on how you spend your time and deal with household problems or work challenges. For that reason alone, it's valuable to imagine yourself acting as you would if you were just a child: free spirited, boundless, uncontrollably creative, and unafraid to try new things.

YOUR CHALLENGE: Act as if you were three years old for a day (or at least part of a day). Jump on your bed, be extremely picky about what you eat, and tackle the day the same way you did when you were three years old. Share the experience with a friend for bonus points.

 CONVERGENT

6. SET AN UNREALISTIC GOAL

Pressure can be a debilitating thing, particularly for creative efforts. But an interesting thing happens if you give yourself even more pressure, to the point of making something you want to do seem impossible: All doubts, fears, and second-guessing go out the window. This freedom to *try*, in turn, makes a great environment for creative thinking, because you know the end result isn't likely to happen, so you'll give it everything you've got, knowing you're going to fail regardless of what you do. You may even surprise yourself by actually achieving the impossible.

YOUR CHALLENGE:

Set an unrealistic goal for yourself today. An unrealistic goal could be to come up with 1,000 ideas in one minute, to write 20,000 words by lunch, or to talk with a friend for 13 hours without stopping.

7. REVERSE-BRAINSTORM

Brainstorming is a helpful way to explore how ideas are connected, by drawing them out and seeing how they relate to one another. So what's a reverse brainstorm? It's a way to explore how seemingly unrelated ideas might be connected. By uncovering everything that's *not* associated with something you want to do, you uncover things you may have otherwise overlooked by being too intently focused on what you *do* want to do.

For example: if you wanted to reverse-brainstorm how to write a book, you would think of all the ideas related to not writing a book, such as:

- Not buying a notebook or pen,
- Not thinking of story lines,
- Not sitting down to write, etc.

YOUR CHALLENGE: Reverse what you
want to do (e.g., not write a book, not be more creative, not learn a new skill) and list out what it would take to make that happen (not buying tools to write, being as boring as possible, not asking for help, etc.). Then reverse the ideas you come up with to see if any stand out as solutions to what you originally wanted to do.

8. THINK BIG TO SMALL

If you stop to think about all of the tiny parts that make up any one thing, you could be thinking about it for quite some time. There are almost an infinite number of things that influence and impact any larger thing, right down to atoms and smaller molecules. A computer, for example, looks like a big hunk of metal and glass, but if you look closer, moving your way down from the big things to the tiniest parts that make the computer up, you start to see how a computer is really many smaller things combined to make something bigger. A computer isn't just a computer: It's metal, glass and plastic, screws, springs, wires, copper, ink, electricity, and so much more. How those small parts come together to make the bigger parts is what matters, but how often do we take time to think about that fact?

YOUR CHALLENGE: Pick something in your life that seems simple on its face. Make a list of everything that makes that thing what it is: List all of the smaller parts, then the smaller parts that make up those smaller parts. See how microscopic you can get with the details.

9. FLIP IT AROUND

Artists will often physically turn their artwork upside down to view it in a new way and expose areas where the work could be improved. Doing so allows them to see flaws and other easy-to-overlook details they couldn't see after looking at the artwork right-side up for so long.

The same goes for your everyday lives, including your problems, ideas, and work. You see them "right-side up" for so long that you can't see them in any other way. By flipping your perspective upside down, you expose yourself to a new way of viewing the same old stuff. If you can physically change your perspective—by sitting on your head, or flipping something you're looking at upside down—you'll notice things you never did before as a result of the altered perspective.

YOUR CHALLENGE:

Find a way to flip your work or perspective upside down today. Use a camera to shoot upside down, draw things upside down on paper, or physically sit upside down for a short amount of time. See what stands out as a result of the altered view.

10. FREE-WRITE FOR 5 MINUTES

Free-writing allows you to bypass the usual critical thinking in your brain that runs rampant during the day. You know that little voice in the back of your head? The one that doubts any creative ideas you have, and tells you when you can or can't do something? Free-writing—writing without worrying over what you're writing or how well you're writing it—works in a way that silences the little voice in your head. The simple act of writing aimlessly, without regard for spelling or grammar, allows you to capture your thoughts before your brain has time to filter them, meaning creative ideas have a better chance of bubbling out.

YOUR CHALLENGE:

Write as fast and detailed as you possibly can for just 5 minutes. It doesn't matter what you write about. Write without worrying about spelling or grammar. Just write anything that comes to mind for at least 5 minutes.

11. PRETEND YOU'RE A CARTOON

For cartoon characters, the laws of the real world don't apply. In a cartoon world, heavy things can be picked up effortlessly, appearances can change in a blink of an eye, and anything becomes possible with a clap of the hands or the press of a magic button. What would it be like if you and I lived in such a world? Research has shown that simply imagining yourself in a situation where the rules of regular life don't apply can greatly increase your creativity. By imagining yourself living as a cartoon, you allow your imagination to pursue the childlike ideas that creativity thrives on. As a cartoon character, you can think of interesting ways to solve problems and spend your time—almost anything is possible. By imagining how cartoon-you would act, you can link your imaginative findings to the real world and uncover ways to be more creative in real life.

YOUR CHALLENGE: Imagine that you live in a cartoon world. What would you do? How would you behave? How would your actions impact everyone around you? Spend the day (or part of the day) living in your cartoon world and thinking of how that type of life relates to your real, noncartoon one.

12. DANCE

Any type of physical exertion has been shown to improve thinking ability, even when the movement is only moderate, such as moving your shoulders back and forth or tapping your foot. In one study conducted by researchers from Rhode Island College, scientists found that small amounts of exercise can boost creative potential both during and after the exercise is performed. Another study, conducted by Joan C. Gondola of Baruch College, showed that dancing specifically improves creativity. So it seems that one of the best ways to get a creative boost is to get your body moving with a little dancing.

YOUR CHALLENGE:

Set a timer for 5 to 10 minutes, then dance. Wiggle your arms, do the twist, or simply get up and jump around; anything to get your body moving however you can. Make it even more fun by inviting a friend or coworker to dance along with you.

13. FIND "INVISIBLE GORILLAS"

It's easy to get too focused on a specific task you're doing and miss otherwise obvious things due to your selective attention. Harvard researchers Christopher Chabris and Daniel Simons call these things "Invisible Gorillas." They suggest that our ability to intensely focus on any single thing is great for being productive, but it limits our ability to notice anything just outside whatever our attention is on. As they discovered, "when we're focused on one task, we're noticing and paying attention to a lot less than we really think."

To expand our thinking, we should actively look for "Invisible Gorillas" at any given moment.

YOUR CHALLENGE:

Take a minute to stop and think about all of the things going on around you that you haven't noticed. Spot ten things you didn't notice until this very moment. Challenge a friend to do the same and see who can reach ten hard-to-notice things faster.

14. CHANGE WHAT'S FAMILIAR

It's easy to become overly familiar with things you are used to. For example: you know that if we approach a door, it should open or close when pulled or pushed. Embracing the world as is makes life easier to go through, but that familiarity doesn't do much for your ability to imagine new possibilities.

To spur your creativity, ask yourself what would happen if one or more parts of everyday life changed. What would doors look like if you had to laugh at them to open or close them? How would you wear hats if they were all made of concrete? What would books look like if they were written entirely with big blue or yellow markers? Imagining changes in what we're familiar with allows us to view them in new and intriguing ways.

YOUR CHALLENGE:

Think of the strangest change you could make to something in everyday life but still have things work as normal. Find one person to share your idea of change with, explaining it in detail, and see his or her response.

15. DO SOMETHING COMPLETELY DIFFERENT

In his book *Smarter Than You Think*, author Clive Thompson explores the importance of "cognitive diversity." This type of diversity simply means the act of doing something differently than what you do regularly. (Cognitive diversity could mean meeting for coffee with an old friend you haven't seen in a long time, or visiting a new restaurant in town.) Thompson explains that the reason diverse experiences are so important is because they stimulate areas of your brain that have been less than active, while at the same time giving the more active parts a mental break. It's the combination of mental stimulation and rest that allows creative insights to spark in your brain. Put simply: to have new ideas, you have to encounter new ways of thinking. New experiences allow you to do just that.

YOUR CHALLENGE:

Find something new you can do today. Pick up a guitar or other instrument and learn to play a chord, try playing a new sport, attend a local concert, or visit that restaurant you've been meaning to try. Do something different, big or small.

 CONVERGENT

16. CONSTRAIN YOURSELF

Constraints can help you be more creative by finely focusing your attention. Does that seem counterintuitive? Think about it this way: Without constraints, what you think is possible can feel overwhelmingly limitless, which ends up making you feel paralyzed by having to make a decision. On the other hand, constraints force you to decide and take action, even if your ideas don't initially strike you as being all that great. Take Ernest Hemingway, for example: He challenged himself to write a complete story with the constraint of only being allowed to use six words. The famously moving, but slightly grim, result of his exercise in constraint? "For sale: baby shoes, never worn."

YOUR CHALLENGE: Add a major constraint to something you're doing now. Only think in verbs, draw with only rudimentary shapes, or only do things that involve wearing boots. Alternatively for this challenge, think like Ernest Hemingway and write six stories using only six words each.

17. YES, AND TWENTY-FIVE IDEAS

Improv is the act of creating or performing spontaneously. While improvisation is often used in stage theatre, it works great for any activity by framing your thoughts in unique ways that you might otherwise not consider. One of the best improv strategies involves addressing every idea that comes your way by responding to it with "Yes, and . . ." This technique forces you to accept the scenario you are presented with, no matter what. For example: if you are thinking about writing a book, you might find yourself asking whether or not you have anything worth writing about, to which you could respond:

- Yes, and . . . if I write about my own life, it will be original.
- Yes, and . . . because it's my life, I'll have much of the plot already figured out.
- Yes, and . . . I can write about it as if it were a fantasy novel to make it more exciting.

Yes, and . . . can really work.

YOUR CHALLENGE:

First, write down two to four ideas you want to do today or tomorrow, no matter how far-fetched or imaginative they may seem. Then start writing on a new line with the phrase, "Yes, and . . ." finishing the sentence with whatever comes to mind first. Repeat the process until you've written twenty-five lines for each idea.

18. EXPLAIN SOMETHING COMPLEX TO A CHILD

Children tend to have a simplified perspective of the world because they haven't been exposed to the various rules, constraints, and norms that make grown-up life so complex. As a result, talking to a child means you have to really think about what you're trying to say and "dumb it down" as clearly as you can. By considering how you'd explain something to a child, you give yourself the perfect opportunity to think differently about the topic. Breaking down difficult subjects as you would when talking with a child can be an effective way of thinking about things in new and valuable ways.

YOUR CHALLENGE:

Try to explain something complex—a project you're working on, a dream you had, or an experience you recently had—in a way even a young child could understand. If possible, explain it to a real child, in person.

19. PICTURE THE DETAILS

Our brains naturally group things together to simplify whatever we're looking at or thinking about. For example: when you imagine a pair of sunglasses, you likely see or imagine a solid object, but in reality, what you're seeing is thin glass connected to metal or plastic, bright or dark colors, possible reflections on the lenses or frames themselves, and so on. While the concept of "sunglasses" seems like a simple thing, it's actually many little parts grouped together to form something larger. By imagining the physical details (only the things you can see) of any one thing, you force yourself to really look at the object or topic in ways you might usually not.

YOUR CHALLENGE:

Look up for a moment and note the first thing you see. Write down every possible detail you can about that one object. Focus on shapes, colors, textures, shadows, and the smaller parts.

20. GO FOR A WALK

Walking in an open space encourages creative insight by activating the parts of your brain associated with free thinking, according to science. One study from Marily Oppezzo, a Stanford Post Doctoral Scholar, and Daniel Schwartz, a professor at Stanford Graduate School of Education, demonstrated that the simple act of walking can dramatically increase your thinking ability. Walking allows your brain to get into a mode of thinking that's ideal for creativity: not too focused, but not too wildly free either. As Henry David Thoreau once wrote: "Methinks that the moment my legs begin to move, my thoughts begin to flow . . ."

YOUR CHALLENGE: It's simple enough to go for a walk. This challenge is to find somewhere you can go that is open (without a ceiling) and preferably green with shrubs or trees (for added mood benefits), and walk for a minimum of 10 minutes.

21. STICK YOUR HEAD IN SOMETHING WACKY

No, not literally. Instead, metaphorically "bury" yourself in something you would typically consider to be strange or odd. By exploring things outside of what you usually consider to be "normal," you allow yourself to bump against new ways of thinking. To give yourself new perspective:

- Listen to an entire album of music you typically wouldn't listen to.
- Read something you think might be strange.
- Do something you otherwise wouldn't regularly do.

YOUR CHALLENGE: Immerse yourself in something different. Click on a wacky or odd-sounding link in your Facebook or Twitter feed. Borrow an article of clothing you wouldn't normally wear. Watch a complete movie that looks like it will be terrible or that has poor ratings.

22. EXPAND YOUR FOCUS FRAME

When you're focused, you see exactly what matters most and little else. Focus is great for productivity, but it hinders your ability to be open and aware of inspiration. Imagine a painter who spends all her time thinking about the painting itself, but not how the painting will be framed and how the frame will affect the way the painting will be viewed. To be more creative, you must force yourself to see what's outside of your focus frame. The best way to do that, according to research from Stanford University, is to step back and ask questions about what you're thinking about. Questions like:

- What around me right now is affecting how I'm thinking?
- If I were anywhere else right now, how would my thinking change?
- How could changing one thing about where I'm at now influence my ideas?

YOUR CHALLENGE:

Take a moment to think about what you're doing right now, including your body position, breathing, and any movement. Now expand your focus by asking yourself: "If I were outside of my body, what would I see? What's around me right now that I might not be fully aware of?"

23. FLIP YOUR ASSUMPTIONS

Your brain is making assumptions all the time. Assumptions about your actions, the people around you, and decisions you make. Think about the weather outside and you will quickly assume how long it would take you to travel anywhere, or what clothing would be best to wear for the day. You don't need to think very hard about those things because your brain makes all the assumptions for you—sometimes correctly but more often than not incorrectly, believe it or not. By purposefully flipping your assumptions on their head, you allow yourself to be more fully aware of what they are and whether or not they're justified. To consciously flip an assumption, you also uncover new perspectives in whatever you're thinking about. As an example: we can assume it's impossible to create a painting without proper painting supplies. To flip that assumption would mean we could paint masterpieces using anything around us, like painting food condiments on paper plates, or using tap water with dirt and sticks to "paint."

YOUR CHALLENGE:

Come up with at least four assumptions you have by thinking of things you believe to be *not true*. Then flip the assumptions around by thinking about what proof you would need to make those assumptions *true*.

24. CREATE A NEW DESIGN

Ideas come in many different shapes, sizes, and levels of complexity, but those designed for visual appeal (like advertisements, book covers, or posters) are made to convey a message as simply as possible. Yet, how often do you find yourself looking at the design of something and questioning why it is the way it is? To think creatively, we should make time to think about the creative decisions others have made. Asking questions such as: Why did the designer decide to use a certain color, pattern, gender, or character for his work? Asking these types of questions—and thinking about the possible answers—allows you to think about visuals you take for granted.

YOUR CHALLENGE: Find an advertisement, packaging, book, or some other visually designed object that you can evaluate. Spend 10 to 15 minutes thinking about the decisions behind the design and drawing an alternative. Get extra points by challenging a friend to do the same, then compare after time is up.

25. MEDITATE

Sitting quietly for 5 to 20 minutes and simply thinking can be hard to do, particularly if you haven't tried doing it before. But meditating like this has been shown to create space in your mind for new ideas. Researchers from Wake Forest University School of Medicine—Fadel Zeidan, Susan K. Johnson, Zhanna David, Paula Goolkasian, and Bruce J. Diamond—have found this to be true: Just 20 minutes of meditation can benefit your ability to focus and think creatively, even if you've never had any formal meditation training. The artist Frederick Franck said it best: "We need a way to detach ourselves from an environment constantly bombarding us with noise, agitation, and visual stimuli." Meditation allows you to do just that.

YOUR CHALLENGE:

Find a quiet place you can sit for up to 30 minutes, set a timer, and try your best to simply sit and meditate by letting your thoughts flow. Focus your mind on your thoughts as they go wherever they want, unguided. Stay seated the entire time.

26. EXPLORE USING YOUR SENSES

Have you ever smelled, tasted, heard, or felt something familiar, only to be reminded of another time you smelled, tasted, heard, or felt it before? Your senses are embedded in your memories, making them incredibly powerful for calling up the old days in an instant. To invoke memories that can help you associate where you are now with a past experience, you might:

- Smell a familiar scent
- Hear an old song
- Remember a time you visited somewhere unique

Jay Sanguinetti from the University of Arizona demonstrated the value of the mind in lab experiments, concluding that our brains sense things on levels we aren't even aware of. By connecting something from the here and now to a memory of a time in the past, your mind becomes capable of comparing the different situations in order to generate new ideas. For example: smelling a familiar scent can remind you of somewhere you went when you were younger but haven't been back to for a while, sparking an idea for an exciting weekend trip.

YOUR CHALLENGE:

Think of something you did yesterday or earlier today and the senses associated with it. How did you feel? What did you smell? Did you taste something unique? Focus on the senses, then think of other times you had those same sense experiences and what the different experiences had in common.

27. DREAM UP 100 SCENARIOS

Linus Pauling, American chemist, author, and educator, once said that "the best way to get a good idea is to have lots of ideas." Modern research has shown that Pauling was onto something: The more ideas you have, the more likely it is that one or more of them will be good. Researcher Alfredo Muñoz Adánez of the Complutense University of Madrid found that the more ideas produced to solve a problem, the better the overall quality of ideas. By thinking of many ideas, you mentally broaden the scope of what's possible, ultimately forcing yourself to think in clever ways to come up with ideas that stand out.

YOUR CHALLENGE: Set a timer for 10 minutes and list at least 100 ideas for something you aren't doing right now, but could be. Anything goes, as long as all of the ideas are realistic.

28. START WITH AN ENDING

If you were going to write a novel, you'd probably start your plot at the beginning. But it turns out that method might not always be the most creative approach. Edgar Allan Poe knew this—he would write his stories with the ending first. Having the ending written out allowed Poe to work within a fixed structure toward a clear objective. When you start a task or project at the end (even if it's just an imagined end) then work your way backwards toward the beginning, you're inclined to finish without feeling stuck or unmotivated since the ending has already been declared. What better way to get something done than by starting from the completed task?

YOUR CHALLENGE: Imagine how your ideal end of the day looks (as realistically as possible). Ask yourself what simple steps it would take to get from what you're imagining to wherever you are now. Work backwards within your imagination to outline each step it would take to get from there to here, writing them down to ensure you don't miss a step. Then take that first step to make it happen.

29. PACKAGE YOURSELF

Things are easier to understand when you can mentally relate them to other things using metaphors. The metaphor can also help you get a different perspective on your subjects. This new way of thinking inevitably leads to creative insights about the object and how you describe it, even if the thing you're describing is yourself. For example: comparing yourself to a toy doll or action figure makes you look at yourself in terms of generalizations and unique attributes.

YOUR CHALLENGE: Think about what you would want your packaging to look like if you were a toy sold in a toy store. What would it say on your box? What features would you come with? What would set your packaging apart from others?

30. GET STRANGELY CURIOUS

According to research led by Charan Ranganath at the University of California, Davis, unique parts of our brain related to memory and pleasure become active when we become overly curious. Curiosity releases chemicals in the brain such as dopamine, which leads to feelings of reward and pleasure (it also happens to help strengthen memories). Ranganath's research also showed that the effects of curiosity are long lasting. That means you're more likely to feel good about a situation and remember information if you feel curious. The increase in memory and mental stimulation is a great way to foster creativity and connect thoughts.

YOUR CHALLENGE: Spend the next 10 or more minutes asking yourself odd questions about whatever is around you now in order to increase your curiosity. Ask questions like: What if vending machines had a "surprise me" button on them? Why don't sheep wear socks? What if windows were made of water? Or: Why do fish swim right-side up if they can face any direction they want underwater?

 CONVERGENT

31. EMULATE INSPIRATION

One of the quickest ways to learn how to do something is to emulate others. For example: children emulate their parents in order to learn how to behave, and novices emulate experts to learn a new skill. What better way to think more creatively than by emulating someone who inspires you? The challenge is not only to emulate others (or the work they've created) but to think about the decisions behind the behaviors. By spending even a small amount of time thinking like you imagine those who inspire you would think, you unlock new perspectives on how to reach your goals.

YOUR CHALLENGE: Think of someone in your life who inspires you and try to emulate how you imagine he or she would behave for a day. Alternatively, find a work of art that inspires you and try to re-create it, thinking about the decisions behind every element of it and why they were made.

 DIVERGENT

32. CHAT WITH A NONCREATIVE

Everyone has a unique perspective on the world. Learning more about different perspectives is especially valuable because they allow you to see your own biases in how you think and what you're familiar with. One of the best ways to understand different perspectives is to talk with a person who has one. Of course, conversations with like-minded friends and coworkers can make you feel good too, but to see the biggest shift in perspective, talk with those who have perspectives that might be the opposite of your own.

YOUR CHALLENGE: Think of the people in your life who you find uncreative. Meet with them today and talk about their perspectives on what it means to be creative and how it might be different (or similar) to your own. Their answers might surprise you.

33. EXPLORE WHAT DOESN'T COME NEXT

Every action has an equal and opposite reaction, and the same is true of ideas. Thinking of any one thing can immediately lead to thinking of another, opposite thing, even if you don't consciously realize it. For example: thinking of something hot might also mean you're thinking of something cold. We know what "hot" means by explicitly contrasting it to "cold," and vice versa. These unexplored relationships can lead to creative insights in the form of alternatives and new contexts. Thinking about what *isn't* readily connected to what you're doing at any given moment, for example, is a great way to spark new ideas and give you different perspectives.

YOUR CHALLENGE:

Think about what you're doing now, or something you'll be doing later today. Then think about what isn't expected to come immediately after that thing, or the next. How does knowing what doesn't come next affect what does?

34. CAMOUFLAGE SOMETHING AROUND YOU

Imagining objects in different environments is one way to easily expand your perceptions of them. Placing an object somewhere it normally wouldn't be makes it easier to spot even the smallest attributes you take for granted or don't usually think about. By imagining things in unique environments, you also have to imagine how the changing circumstance would affect the thing itself. To take things a step further, you could imagine that the objects need to match their surroundings, via camouflage.

YOUR CHALLENGE:

Look around you now, and pick one or two objects. Imagine what would happen if the objects were placed somewhere unique and had to be camouflaged there. How would the changed environment affect not only how they look, but function?

35. BE PURPOSEFULLY BORING

When you're bored, your unrestrained consciousness is free to work through problems, generate ideas, and imagine possibilities. One study from the University of Central Lancashire bored participants silly by making them copy down phone numbers from a phone book. Compared to a different group of people who did not have to do the boring task, creative thinking was significantly greater in those who were instructed to copy phone numbers. The study concluded that daydreaming caused by boredom acted as a creative catalyst, prompting more original thinking as a result of having just the right amount of mental freedom to do so. Boredom, it turns out, can be a seriously great way to ignite creativity in your life.

YOUR CHALLENGE:

Set a timer for 15 minutes and find something boring you can do. For example, wash and re-wash dishes, sort and re-sort clothes or stacks of paper, or organize a library.

36. BUILD REMOTE ASSOCIATIONS

Research from neuroscientists like that of University of Bristol's Paul Howard-Jones has shown that we think creatively when we're forced to find connections between ideas. In one study, Howard-Jones asked participants to write a story based on three random words. The study showed that those participants given three seemingly unrelated words (like fish, paper, and wheel), came up with more creative stories than participants who were given more obviously associated words (like fish, water, and bowl). Forcing your brain to find remote associations between ideas when those associations aren't easy to see, can help spark your creativity.

YOUR CHALLENGE: Keeping this page bookmarked with your thumb or a bookmark, flip to a separate page in this book. Pick one word at random from the page you turn to, then turn again to a different page and note the next word you see first. Write down all the different ways that the two random words can be connected.

37. GO UPSIDE DOWN

Much of what we think (and how we think it) is influenced by our perspective and shaped by our experiences. To be more creative, you should seek to change your perspectives often. Physically changing your perspective, for example, can lead to insights because of the literally new, unique perspective it gives you. Michael Michalko, famed creative writer, explains: "What Copernicus [and] Darwin really achieved was not the discovery of a new theory, but a fertile new point of view." Your point of view matters, and changing yours can invite insights you otherwise might have never seen.

YOUR CHALLENGE: Find a place where you can sit upside down for a short while and take notes about how the change in perspective affects your opinion of what you see. Or use a camera to take a picture of a place where you spend a lot of time, then flip the picture upside down and note the things you never noticed before, or how what you're used to looks suddenly different.

38. CREATE AN IDEA CHAIN

We tend to think only in terms of ideas that are related to one another, which can often lead us to thinking in a repetitive cycle. Thankfully, there are ways of breaking our cycles of thinking. An idea chain is one such way. To create an idea chain, first think of two related words, writing them down with a sizable space between them. Then, focusing on the first word only, write the next word that comes to mind right next to it. Keep writing words like this to create a chain connecting the first word to the last word. For example: if you wanted to do something fun today, your chain might start like this: "Fun _____ _____ _____ _____ Today." By the end of the exercise that same chain could look like this: "Fun Dance Celebration Birthday Cake Today," which could lead you to the idea of having a faux birthday celebration for fun today.

YOUR CHALLENGE: Write down something you want to do today, using only two words and leaving a large gap between them. Look at the first word and write next to it the first thing that comes to mind. Then think of related words for the second word, repeating the process until you reach the last word.

39. STORYBOARD YOURSELF

Placing yourself into an imaginary role makes it easier to think of wild ideas that might not make sense in the real world. Role daydreaming like this is great for fighting boredom, but it can help spark creative ideas too. For this challenge, you're going to imagine your life as though it were a movie, but only at the "storyboarding" stage. Storyboarding involves drawing very simple frames of what's going to happen in the movie, one scene at a time. By drawing scenes of what you want to happen—whether it's solving a problem or doing something exciting today—you give your imagination just enough context to fill in the gaps.

YOUR CHALLENGE: First, draw a few squares or "frames" to create your storyboard. In the first frame, draw yourself drawing your storyboard. The last frame can be anything. Use your imagination to fill in all the empty frames between the first and last one, whether it's four empty frames or thirty.

 EMERGENT

40. LEAVE IT UNDONE

Ernest Hemingway would famously stop working in the middle of his writing if he felt he was doing a good job. Doing so would help spark new ideas out of him whenever he sat down to continue writing. Can you imagine what Shakespeare's plays would be like if they were left unfinished? Or what it would be like if all of the greatest artists throughout history never finished their paintings? When something is left incomplete, certain parts of the brain activate in an attempt to imagine it completed. By purposefully stopping a story in the middle of a sentence, or a drawing halfway through, or a project just before it's finished, you give your brain a natural drive to try and finish or resolve it. Leaving something undone, it turns out, is a surprisingly effective way to get your ideas flowing.

YOUR CHALLENGE: Think about something you need to get done today or tomorrow, even if it's something you're doing now (like reading this book). Once you start to feel like you're making good progress on that thing, stop and walk away. Think about what you would do to complete the task, then actually sit down to continue it awhile later.

41. CREATE SOMETHING TERRIBLE

The idea of perfectionism can leave us feeling paralyzed. We might not take up a new hobby or interest because we feel like we won't be good enough at it, for example. On the other hand, spending a few minutes to make something purposefully terrible can be empowering. If you start something with the full intent of making it bad to begin with, you lose the fear of failing or falling short of the ideal, which allows you to tackle the task more comfortably. After all, it's difficult to make something that isn't terrible if your goal to begin with was to make it just that.

YOUR CHALLENGE: Create something purposefully terrible. Write a horrible twenty-page poem, or take some truly bad photos and turn them into an album, or make a bad painting with mismatched colors and impossible-to-interpret shapes.

 DIVERGENT

42. TIME TRAVEL

In the imaginary future, if you can imagine it, it can happen. Because it's imaginary, the rules and constraints of reality don't have to fully apply. Resources can be cheaper, you can instantly transport to other places, and robots can help you do anything you need to do. Imagining yourself in a future scenario means you'll be able to imagine an alternative way of thinking about your life and problems. This imaginary scenario can bring to light all of the things you may have otherwise been overlooking in your current situation.

YOUR CHALLENGE:

Draw or write about yourself living in an imaginary future, a minimum of 1,000 years from now. What's different? How do you spend your time? What do you miss about the past?

43. FOCUS ON FIRST PRINCIPLES

Our brains like to think by analogy: comparing one thing to another. Thinking in ways other than by analogy allows you to see things in different ways. One such way to think is by using "First Principles." This approach requires you to look at the fundamental facts around something, then imagine how you could build from those basic principles.

For example: if you wanted to write a book, the first principles would be the words, narration, and structure. While most stories include characters, there's nothing in the first principles of a book that says you have to include them, therefore you could say that you're writing a book about something (like time travel) that doesn't include any characters.

YOUR CHALLENGE:

Think about one aspect of your life—something you want to do, a project you're working on, or a problem you're trying to solve—and look at what the fundamental truths or first principles are around it. Write them down, then write down how you would accomplish what you want to do based on *only* those core truths and nothing more.

 AESTHETIC

44. IMAGINE YOURSELF FAR AWAY

There's a theory in psychology known as "construal level theory," which states that the more distant we are from something, the more likely we are to think of it in abstract ways. This abstraction is great for creativity, as it makes it easier to imagine possibilities without limits. In psychological research led by Lile Jia of Indiana University, researchers were able to show that the effects of simply imagining yourself being far away from where you really are allows you to view your life in a more abstract—and therefore creative—way.

YOUR CHALLENGE:

Draw or write as though you were far away from where you really are right now. Where would you be? How would being in that distant place affect what you're doing at the moment?

45. HELP SOMEONE ELSE

According to researchers at the University of Missouri-Columbia, our modern-day brains grew to be the size they are as a result of social problem solving. By thinking of what others might do, our ancestors were able to keep themselves safe and happy. The researchers explain: "The most exceptional of our mental gifts involves understanding what is going on in other people's minds." That same mode of thinking is powerful for creativity, where we can step away from our own perspective of the world in order to think in terms of someone else's. Seeing the world from someone else's perspective is powerful for gaining insights, and there's no better way to gain that perspective than by attempting to help someone with a project or problem.

YOUR CHALLENGE:

Find a friend, coworker, or family member who is working on a project or has a clear problem. Offer to help them work on it for a few hours or until it's complete or resolved.

46. WRITE A 100-LINE POEM

One way to jolt your creative thinking is to constrain yourself to one method of expression or action. Constraining yourself can force you to think in ways you otherwise wouldn't, by exploring possibilities to help achieve the task within the bounds you set.

Look no further than the haiku form of poetry as a good example of this in action. In haiku, the poet is restricted to writing just three lines, following the pattern of five syllables, then seven, then five again. By restricting themselves to this pattern of writing, poets are forced to think creatively to come up with poems that meet the requirements of the format.

YOUR CHALLENGE: Write a 100-line poem using a pattern or other constraints, like starting with one word, then adding one additional word to each line, or by using a familiar pattern like haiku until you've written thirty-three haikus to form one 100-line poem.

47. BECOME A SECRET AGENT

When you imagine yourself in situations that rely on creativity, you allow your brain to come up with solutions and answers in ways that don't have to rely on reality. We see this in children all the time: When they aren't sure of how something works, or when they're simply bored, they use their imagination to come up with solutions. As author and creativity expert Sir Ken Robinson explains, ". . . young children are wonderfully confident in their own imaginations. Most of us lose this confidence as we grow up." The more difficult the situation is to manage with our imaginations, the more creative we're likely to get, which is why pretending to be a secret agent for a day can be a strong motivator for thinking creatively.

YOUR CHALLENGE: Spend the day acting like a secret agent. Nobody can know you're an agent (that's the "secret" part), so your mission is to make it through the day without blowing your cover. Your goal throughout the day should be to act as suave and dangerous as you imagine a secret agent would be, without blowing your cover. This book will now self-destruct in 10 seconds.

48. BACKTRACK

If you look back at the last few hours of your day (or the last few days of your week), you're undoubtedly going to notice some patterns in how you acted. We call these patterns of behavior "routine." Understanding your personal routine is a great way to identify opportunities for trying new things and exposing yourself to new perspectives on your life. By working backwards from where you are now to where you were yesterday or last week, you can identify themes in your routine that may have influenced you without you even realizing it. If you write down those themes or routine elements, you can then more easily outline which areas can be changed and which are the most valuable as they are.

YOUR CHALLENGE: Think about all the major things you did in the last few hours or last few days and any themes in your routine. Note how areas of your routine impacted everything that came after them. Star any areas where your routine is getting dull or overly repetitive, then think about what would happen if you changed any one of them.

49. DRAW WITH YOUR OTHER HAND

When we draw (even just doodling) our brains have to control the movement of our hand, and also think about what we're drawing before we draw it. Of course, if you're talented enough, you can create strikingly realistic drawings. However, if you try to draw using your non-dominant hand (left hand for right-handed people, right for left-handed) the signals between what you see and what you're trying to draw don't match up quite as well, since the motor functions in your brain aren't trained to perform that way. As a result, doodling with your opposite hand can lead you to create drawings that are more fluid and abstract. Abstract images happen to be a great way to develop a creative eye and spot details in how your perception affects what you're drawing.

YOUR CHALLENGE:

Spend the next 15 minutes trying to draw something around you using only your non-dominant hand. To make this extra fun, invite a friend or coworker to draw with you, then compare drawings.

 EMERGENT

50. GET SOME SUN

Researchers at the Washington University School of Medicine tested the mental effect sunlight has on the brain. They found that sunlight not only improved mood in participants (by causing certain chemicals to be produced in the body), but it also improved their cognitive thinking ability overall. If you want to feel more creative and be happier, the research shows, working under the sun can help you to do just that. There's even technology that creates the same type of light right inside your home or office, called "blue light boxes," so you don't have to get up from your desk to reap the benefits sunlight offers your brain.

YOUR CHALLENGE:

Spend up to an hour working under the sun (or near a natural light) today. Be sure to drink plenty of water as you do, so you don't get overheated, which is likely to produce the opposite result of what you're hoping for.

51. ANSWER, "WHAT WOULD ___ DO?"

Imagining how your problems or situations look from another person's perspective is a powerful way of gaining new insights. By imagining how someone else might approach the same situation you're in—whether it's solving a problem, working on a project, or figuring out how to spend a Saturday afternoon—you're free to imagine things in ways you might not usually think of them. For example: if you're shy, imagining how a socially outgoing friend might act at a neighborhood gathering means you're more likely to imagine yourself doing socially outgoing things too. This imagined perspective broadens your horizons and encourages creative thinking.

YOUR CHALLENGE: Think of one or two people in your life whom you look up to, then try to imagine what they would do if they were in your situation right now. Imagine all of the small details of what they would do. Then imagine what would happen if you acted that way too.

52. DRAW A MAP WITHOUT LANDMARKS

Our brains absorb a lot more information than we realize. Researchers from the University of Arizona found this to be the case when they showed study participants images with blurry objects just outside the center of vision. Using brain scan imagery, the researchers demonstrated that even if we're not consciously aware of everything going on around us, parts of our brains "light up" with activity related to those tiny details; whether it's things at our peripheral vision, sounds we don't consciously hear, or smells we become so familiar with that we fail to realize their strength after a while (like wearing our favorite cologne or perfume). More often than not, all of the small details around us are recorded as non-obvious sensory experiences related to sound, texture, light, smells, and more.

YOUR CHALLENGE: Draw a map to somewhere you visit often, but rather than giving explicit directions or using memorable markers for how to get to the location, try to think of (and draw) only small details you consciously haven't tried thinking of before. Use small details to represent what you see, smell, hear, feel, or otherwise encounter on your journey from where you are now to the place you are mapping.

53. WRITE IT OUT IN STAGES

We tend to focus on the end result of things: If we want to write a book, we envision what the completed book might look like. If we want to make a movie, we imagine it playing to an audience. The problem with thinking in such a result-oriented way is that doing so makes the actual work—of writing a book or creating a movie—seem more complex than it really is. Instead, you should acknowledge that anything you want to do requires many small steps, not one large leap. By thinking about the small steps required to tackle any challenge, you actually simplify the process creatively.

YOUR CHALLENGE:

Write one sentence explaining something you want to do within the next month. Then, write what the first step to pursuing it might be (whether you've already started or not). Beneath that line write one thing you need to do before the first thing. Repeat the process until you are clear about what steps you need to take.

54. DRAW YOUR FACE UPSIDE DOWN

When we look at a face, we see only very specific features: the shape and location of eyes, the bulge of a nose, or the curve of lips. As a result, if you and I were tasked with drawing a face from memory, the face you draw would look similar to mine, regardless of our artistic abilities. Like drawing faces, our minds have set symbols for nearly everything in our lives, from how automobiles should look to how the doors on buildings should appear. When we flip any of these things upside down, our brains have to struggle to spot the features they're used to seeing. Viewing familiar things from a new perspective (like being upside down) is an effective way to help you notice all the details you usually take for granted.

YOUR CHALLENGE: Find a mirror and something to draw with, then spend the next 10 minutes drawing a detailed portrait of your face upside down. If possible, use a photo you can flip upside down as reference. Note the areas you struggle to draw most and why the change in perspective makes them so difficult to draw.

55. GET 20 MINUTES OF EXTRA SLEEP

Extra sleep (as little as 20 minutes) allows your brain to work uninhibited. Rather than fighting with the constant bombardment of new information it usually gets—in the form of sounds, sights, tastes, and other stimuli—the brain can process and sort information undisturbed during sleep. Research has shown that the calming effects of the chemical serotonin, primarily produced in the body during sleep, strengthen creative networks in the brain. Additional research from Cambridge University has shown that a good night of sleep or a brief 20-minute nap clears away clutter in the brain that restricts new connections from occurring.

YOUR CHALLENGE: Set aside 20 extra minutes today to take a nap or for going to bed early. Ensure that where you're resting is quiet and dark. If you have trouble falling asleep, consider using sleep aids like the sound of crickets chirping or a sleep mask.

56. SPEND A DAY SMALLER

By imagining that you or something in your life has changed size dramatically, you start to think in terms you otherwise might not. It's only when you stop to consider the effects of such a significant change that you can utilize the imagined scenario to your advantage. If you were to imagine yourself as being 1,000 times taller, suddenly how you go about your day-to-day life is going to change a lot: the clothes you wear and how they're made, where you live, and how you get into buildings (or whether you need to get into them in the first place).

YOUR CHALLENGE: Imagine what you would do today if you were 1,000 times smaller. If you shrank to be that size, how would you spend your time? What interesting things would you do? Spend part of your day today acting as though you really had shrunk to 1,000 times your normal size.

57. ROLE-PLAY SOMEONE YOU KNOW

Imagining yourself as someone else allows your mind to explore possibilities that might not align with how you usually think or behave. This imaginary exercise works wells for a lot of uses because you get to see the world from the perspective of someone who might be more capable, creative, or resourceful than you think you are. Yet when you put yourself in someone else's shoes, you're really relying on your own imagination to connect his or her perceived behaviors with your situation. This means that while you're imagining how someone else might spend his or her time, your own creative ideas are generating the scenario.

YOUR CHALLENGE:

Think of someone you look up to and imagine what it would be like to spend the day as him or her. Focus on how he or she would act when faced with the same issues you face. What makes the person so unique from your perspective?

58. DEFINE 100 STEPS

In his book *Blink*, Malcolm Gladwell cites the research of psychologist Gerd Gigerenzer, who found that we often make snap decisions based on only limited information. One result of our quick judgments is that we tend to view things as being more difficult than they really are. As an example: we think about writing a book and immediately imagine all of the endless writing required to do it. In reality, many things in life are easier than we lead ourselves to believe. By breaking down your tasks into smaller chunks, you can more easily see the domino effect that your actions and decisions create, leading you to reach more of your goals.

YOUR CHALLENGE: Create a list of each of the steps it would take you to achieve one of your dreams or goals in life. Your challenge is to list at least 100 detailed steps in total, no matter how long it takes you to come up with the complete list.

59. REDESIGN TIME

When you think about the word "time," you're likely to imagine a clock. A clock is a universal symbol for representing time because it helps us to manage it. If you look at a clock, you'll notice that they all appear to be very similar, no matter where you are in the world or what time it is. To think creatively, you need to be able to look at everyday objects like clocks and think about why they are the way they are, rather than simply taking them for granted. Have you ever stopped to think about why objects like clocks are the way they are or why they work the way they do? By asking questions about everyday objects, you can develop an eye for the small details that can be modified in order to spark creative ideas.

YOUR CHALLENGE: Spend up to 20 minutes thinking about why clocks look the way they do and drawing your best alternative to modern-day clocks. Challenge a friend to do the same and then compare what you both come up with.

60. STRETCH OUT

Research from Roosevelt University and the University of Copenhagen (among others) has shown that stretching for even a few short minutes helps to release chemicals in the body that relax nerves and improve blood flow. That relaxed state and increase in blood flow helps energize and strengthen your brain by releasing tension, reducing stress, and boosting perceived thinking ability. It helps that physically stretching is a great reflection of mental stretching: reaching out and bending in different ways to push your thinking into new directions.

YOUR CHALLENGE: Take 5 minutes to really stretch out. You can do that standing up or sitting down—simply move your body to loosen your muscles and connective fibers. Then spend another 10 minutes sitting and relaxing while the benefits from all that stretching start to take shape.

 CONVERGENT

61. FIND THE MOST SURPRISING FRAME

In psychological terms, the "framing effect" can influence how we make decisions and brainstorm ideas by changing the frame we view anything in. Think of it like viewing a glass of water as being half-full or half-empty. If you're thirsty, you're likely to feel better about a glass being half-full as opposed to one that is half-empty. By changing the frame of something, you change how it's perceived, how it might be used, how it looks, and ultimately what's possible with it. For example: a cup in a kitchen is ideal for pouring liquids or getting a drink, but take that same cup to the beach (a different frame) and it's suddenly very useful for building sandcastles.

YOUR CHALLENGE: Find one or two objects around you now and imagine them in different frames. Write down all of the different ways the object changes within the new frame. Challenge a friend to do the same exercise and see which of the frames you both come up with is most surprising.

62. REINTERPRET SOMETHING YOU MAKE

Seeing how something can be used in different contexts and for different purposes opens up your mind to a world of possibilities. For example: imagining how a fruit basket could be used as a hat, or how a shoe could be used as a glove or a weapon of self-defense. By reinterpreting the objects around you, you set your attention on the *potential* of things as opposed to simply accepting their current use. Trying to think in this way often opens your focus to notice more around you, as well as see possibilities where others may not.

YOUR CHALLENGE:

Gather a few craft materials—paper, glue, scissors, sticks, markers, scraps of cardstock, anything—and spend just 10 minutes making something basic (a hat, a doll, a poster, anything). The goal isn't to create something specific at the outset, it's to figure out what your creation can become after the fact. What could it be used for? Could it decorate something?

63. ANSWER "WHY NOT?"

Toyota has an interesting approach to exploring possible solutions to problems. They call the technique "5 Whys." By answering "why" then asking "why" four additional times—each time questioning the answer that came just before it—you escape assumptions and logical traps around why something is (or isn't) the way it is. In the 1950s, seeing that a welding robot had stopped on the floor, former Toyota Executive Vice President Taiichi Ohno explored the possibilities: "Why did the robot stop? Its circuit was overloaded. Why was the circuit overloaded? The mechanical bearings on the robot were not sufficiently lubricated. Why were the bearings insufficiently lubricated? The oil pump on the robot wasn't working. Why? The pump was clogged with metal shavings. Why? Because there was no filter on the pump." With that, Toyota improved their welding robots by adding filters to their oil pumps. By taking this approach a step further (and asking "Why not?") you can implore your imagination to explore possibilities you may not have otherwise been able to imagine in the first place.

YOUR CHALLENGE:

Write down one or two questions you have about today or tomorrow (like "Should I go to the gym?" or "Could I start that project I've been meaning to work on?"). Beneath each question, ask yourself "Why not?" and write the first thing that comes to mind. Beneath that line item, again ask "Why not?" then write your answer. Repeat the process three additional times and note what ideas come as a result.

64. KNOW WHAT A PICTURE IS WORTH

A picture is worth a thousand words—but so is any moment in our lives, if we stop and look hard enough. Yet we often go through our days without noticing the tiny details that make up the larger picture of what we remember later on. If we were to stop and notice the details of what we look at, we'd undoubtedly make some interesting discoveries. For example: sitting on a hill overlooking a city, you might see buildings and roads, but if you looked hard enough, you could see paint on the road, light bulbs in the streetlights, shards of glass, gravel, many different colors, the movement of cars, and much more. These details can build connections to new ideas or creative moments.

YOUR CHALLENGE: Find a picture you like—of a person, place, or thing—and set a timer for 6 minutes. Make a list to see just how many small details you can spot in the picture. For an added bonus: have a friend look at the same photo and make his or her own list, then compare after the 6 minutes are up.

65. TAKE A MINI VACATION

Your regular day-to-day life is probably filled with creativity-crushing routine. At home, life is easy to run on autopilot. Away from home, however, you're much more likely to have an impactful experience that sparks creativity because there's little that resembles your regular life. If you've ever traveled to a faraway city or country (or a friend's house) you know just how challenging even the smallest things away from home can be. Something as simple as figuring out how to get a glass of water can become a challenge if you're not in a familiar place. To challenge your way of thinking—and to have more memorable experiences—you don't need to travel all the way to a foreign country, you just need to get away from your daily routine in a way that presents new challenges.

YOUR CHALLENGE:

Set aside some time today, all of tomorrow, or all of another day for a mini vacation. Your vacation could involve traveling to a nearby city, visiting a cafe or museum you've never been to, or staying in bed (literally) all day.

 CONVERGENT

66. WAKE UP 30 MINUTES EARLY

Writer Dorothea Brande proposes an interesting idea for us to consider: Wake up 30 minutes early and jump right into a creative project. By starting a creative task immediately after waking up, we circumvent the internal critic in each of us. The theory Brande proposes is that your conscious editor—that quiet voice in the back of your head that tells you when an idea seems too wild—takes at least 30 minutes to "wake up" after you consciously do. Without that mental critic awake to judge what you want to do, you're more inclined to produce creative ideas.

YOUR CHALLENGE: Set a timer for 30 minutes earlier than you usually wake up tomorrow. Plan a creative activity—or define a problem you need to solve creatively—and when you wake up start immediately on it. No snoozing that alarm, otherwise you'll lose valuable time without your internal critic!

67. ASK AN INSPIRATION FOR INSPIRATION

We tend to seek out things that inspire us for good reason: The right kind of inspiration can provide fuel for original ideas of our own. Now, thanks to the Internet, it's easier than ever to find inspiration. But how often do you look at an inspiration without thinking of the inspiration that inspired it? Behind your inspiration—be that a person, piece of art, idea, or location—lie interesting decisions, fascinating personalities, and unique historical perspectives that can help you ignite your own creative ideas. What ultimately inspired da Vinci to paint the *Mona Lisa* could also have been inspiration for countless other artists to create masterpieces of their own. And we're not talking about the model behind the *Mona Lisa* here, but the drive to paint in the style da Vinci chose, using the colors and angles he did. The inspiration that inspires those who inspire you is worth exploring.

YOUR CHALLENGE: Pick two or three people who inspire you and contact them within the next hour to ask two questions: First, what inspires them? Second, how did they use that inspiration to fuel their own creativity?

68. SPLIT FOCUS WITH DAYDREAMING

Mark Beeman, a cognitive neuroscientist at Northwestern University, says that the best way to have creative insights is to dedicate as much time as possible to focusing on one topic as you do daydreaming about ideas. In an interview with the *New Yorker*, Beeman states: "Your state of attention both before you get a problem and when you're solving it matters." So if you want to be at your creative best, you have to focus on what you want to do long enough before you start the actual work in order to ensure you're covering all the details. Only after you've exhausted thinking of all logistical angles of the task are you free to start daydreaming about possibilities.

YOUR CHALLENGE:

Identify a problem you have that you want to solve creatively, or a creative project you've been meaning to start (or finish). Spend the next 30 minutes (or more) writing an outline of the details around the problem or project. Then set aside an equal amount of time to daydream about the outline you just created.

69. CAPTURE A MOMENT OF MOTION

There is often an energy we overlook when we think. We imagine a tree and it appears to us as a static thing, sitting quietly in a field or cityscape. Yet it's the moments of motion that make an idea feel alive: the rattling of leaves on the tree, the sway of grass around it, or the movement of a passerby running through the park. By focusing on the moments of movement, we see how static ideas connect to other ideas: The wind affects the tree and the grass around it, the movement of legs powers the runner. Recognizing these motions allows you to see ideas in a more energizing way, reminding you to stop and think about the moments of motion that connect ideas you usually envision as standing still in time.

YOUR CHALLENGE: Using your drawing tools of choice, try to capture all the details from a moment of motion. The moment you choose to draw can be anything, as long as it symbolizes the motion of action: cars driving by, someone running, the wind through grass, or something else.

70. DISCONNECT YOURSELF

Research from Stanford neuroscientists Vinod Menon and Daniel Levitin shows that the daily "jibber jabber" of text messages, phone calls, TV advertisements, and other bombarding stimulation takes a toll on our mental state. When our brains are in consuming mode—a result of being overwhelmed by everything coming at us in the day—we don't have enough mental power to enable creation or ideation. The research doesn't lie: Being in a consistent state of information consumption leaves us feeling overwhelmed and unable to think as creatively as we might like. What's the solution? Disconnect and give your brain space to create rather than absorb.

YOUR CHALLENGE: Spend the rest of today (or all of tomorrow) disconnected from anything that can distract you. Disconnect from the Internet, turn off your phone, unplug the TV, forget about reading the news, etc. Dedicate a half of (or a whole) day to be disconnected, think, and relax.

71. CREATE A MOOD BOARD

Anything can spark your imagination. Think of the positive feeling you get while reading a really good book, watching a well-made film, or browsing the Internet for an hour. Unfortunately, we often forget to look at how our various forms of inspiration combine. Yet if we don't put those inspirations together in one place, we lose precious time, energy, and productivity trying to find them again. In the design world, people often create a mood board to help alleviate this issue. A mood board, a physical or digital "board" that shows multiple pieces of inspirational material together, can help spark ideas and create connections between objects whenever you need them most.

YOUR CHALLENGE: Consider the different elements of inspiration in your life and think of how you might gather and combine them in a digital or physical way. Grab photos, quotes of inspiration, colors, even sound bites or videos, and anything else you can use to inspire your brain, then combine them into a board you can reference for future ideas.

72. WRITE YOUR STORY

When you wake up every day and go about your business, do you ever think about what a story for each of those moments would read like? A story has a clear beginning, middle, and end structure to it, but your life might not seem like it in the moment. If you view any single moment as a standalone story, however, you give power to the things that would otherwise go unnoticed. To look at anything in your life as a story (in the old-fashioned sense) is to create a framework from which you are free to explore possibilities and identify what matters most (and what matters least), including things you may be overlooking unconsciously.

YOUR CHALLENGE: Think of a specific moment from your life yesterday: when you woke up, traveled somewhere, met with a friend, or other event. Write a one- to two-page story about it, describing in detail the beginning, middle (or climax of the story), and end. Who or what is the protagonist/antagonist of the moment? What was the conflict in that moment that had to be overcome?

73. VOICE-RECORD IDEAS

There's a lot of value in "thinking out loud," as they say. Having to vocalize your thoughts into something that makes sense (both to say and to hear) can be difficult, as it requires a solid structure that is vastly different than the freeform thinking our brains are naturally using. By vocalizing your thoughts as they occur, your brain has to sort through the necessary information required to turn even the most abstract idea into something that can be translated vocally. If you record yourself explaining your thinking, then play the recording back (creating a type of conversation with yourself), you allow yourself to experience your thoughts in a tangible way.

YOUR CHALLENGE: Spend 1 minute recording yourself talking about the first thing that comes to mind, then another minute playing it back to yourself. Repeat the process five times for a total of 10 minutes with your recorder.

74. DRAW THIRTY CIRCLES

Bob McKim, once a lead at the Stanford Design Program, created a challenge in the '70s that helped students get over the initial hesitation they had around drawing. McKim would hand students a sheet of paper and tell them to draw the person sitting next to them in 30 seconds. By tasking students with creating a drawing in just 30 seconds, McKim found that students wouldn't have time to critique their work, which often led to more creative solutions. A similar exercise used by product design studio IDEO is to take thirty circles drawn on a page and try to make something tangible from the circles (by only drawing inside each of them individually) in just 3 minutes.

YOUR CHALLENGE: Using a single sheet of paper, draw thirty circles of about the same size each (they don't have to be perfect circles!). Set a timer for 3 minutes, then draw inside of the circles to make as many different objects as you can: a wheel, looking down on a coffee cup, a button, and so on.

75. SET ASIDE TIME FOR CREATIVITY

Julia Cameron, author of the bestselling creative help book *The Artist's Way* dedicates 30 minutes each morning to writing. Mozart regularly made time to work in short, one- to two-hour bursts throughout the day. Famous writer Franz Kafka set aside much of the night—from 11 P.M. until 6 A.M.—to write. Blocking out part of your day for the purpose of creative thinking allows new ideas to spark without distraction. If you are looking to be more creative, you need to make time to do it, whether it's an hour a day or 20 minutes a day. Setting aside a specific time for a creative activity makes it more likely to happen.

YOUR CHALLENGE: Set aside time today for a creative activity like writing, painting, or learning something new. Let your friends and family know that you've scheduled some creative time for yourself, then stick to it.

76. CONNECT WITH A DIFFERENT BACKGROUND

Humans are pack animals, in the sense that we prefer to be around people who are like us or who do similar work or have the same interests. While our tendency to form "tribes" is great for making us feel safe and welcomed, it can hinder our ability to think creatively (since all of the perspectives we deal with will be the same as ours). Tim Brown, cofounder of world-renowned product design firm IDEO, suggests you take every opportunity you have to connect with those whose interests are different than yours, in order to gain creative perspectives.

YOUR CHALLENGE: Find someone (online or in your city) who works in a different industry or discipline than you do. Chat together or write to her and ask what inspires and motivates her. Share your perspective and get her opinion on it for added benefits.

77. GO WITHOUT "I" FOR A DAY

Expecting things to follow a fairly structured and predictable flow is called "routine." While structured routines are great for our well-being, they do little to help us see new possibilities or perspectives. By changing any structured part of a day, you force yourself to think in different ways in order to accomplish what would otherwise come naturally for you. Things like only being able to eat blue food, having to start each sentence you speak or write without using the words "I know," or (for this challenge) removing the word "I" from your vocabulary for the day, force you to think about things that would otherwise be easy to ignore.

YOUR CHALLENGE: For the rest of today (or all of tomorrow), try not using the word "I" in anything you speak or write. Instead, find ways to communicate without mentioning "I" and see where the struggle to do so brings about creative solutions.

78. BREAK APART THE STEPS

It's easy to go through the day without considering all the steps of any one task you accomplish. From getting out of bed or eating to driving a car or having a conversation, we view those activities as single actions. But each of those activities requires a number of steps to take place, one at a time, in a specific order. By looking closely at any of the steps required to do any single thing, you can discover ways of improving the process or improving your understanding of the process. These added insights help you acknowledge that even complex activities (like writing a novel, starting a business, or building a house by hand) all involve more simple step-by-step actions that are easier to tackle than you might first imagine.

YOUR CHALLENGE: Write down ten specific things you did yesterday (like eat breakfast, go to school or work, drive or walk home, etc.) then pick one of the activities and break it down into as many steps as possible, noting which steps you never really took the time to think about.

79. DOODLE SOMETHING

Research shows that doodling (no matter how poor the drawing ends up) changes how your brain processes information. Doodling requires you to think about what you're drawing in a unique way as you draw; your brain is tasked with not only managing the perception of what you're drawing as you see it on paper, but also the imagined version you see in your mind. This bridging of what you see and what you imagine leads to stronger interpretations of whatever you doodle . . . even if it's something silly or ambiguous like a product from the future or how you are feeling in any moment.

YOUR CHALLENGE:

Take the next 10 minutes to doodle how you feel right now. No matter how great (or terrible) of an artist you might be, try to create a doodle that captures exactly how you feel. Hang the drawing on your refrigerator for a day.

80. COOK SOMETHING

Cooking encourages you to set your mind onto a series of tasks toward a clear objective. That intense focus—of having all conscious actions and thoughts going through your mind toward a single goal—allows you to enter a zen-like state of thinking. When you cook, the planning and problem-solving parts of your mind become active while the more complex, unconscious parts are free to do what they do best: think sub-consciously. As a result: cooking is a great way to relax your mind, spur on creative ideas, and end up with something to eat to boot.

YOUR CHALLENGE:

Find a new recipe, online or in your favorite recipe book, that you can cook today. Think about how the process of preparing and cooking makes your mind feel. Serve the meal to your friends or family.

81. IMITATE A CONVERSATION

If you've never sat in a public place and imitated talking with someone nearby who was on the phone or simply talking loudly, you're missing out on a great opportunity to use your imagination. Listening to a public conversation taking place, and imagining what your answers or responses would be, can help utilize the parts of your brain relied on for creativity. Think of this as a vocal game of improv, where you have to play along to unexpected situations.

YOUR CHALLENGE: Go to a public place like a cafe or shopping center (alone or with a friend) and see if you can listen in on a public conversation. Take turns quietly "joining" in the conversations you hear as if the person were actually speaking to you.

82. ASK "WHAT COULD HAVE HAPPENED?"

Research from the University of California, Berkeley, Ohio University, and Northwestern University showed that imagining the past as being different than it really was "promotes an expansive processing style that broadens conceptual attention and facilitates performance on creative generation tasks." In other words: imagining what could have happened in the past can encourage you to think more creatively about the future, by creating a chain of events your imagination can easily build from. The benefit works not only in the event you're looking back at, but also in other areas of life.

YOUR CHALLENGE: Think about something that happened to you yesterday or a day before, then imagine what would have happened if things had gone differently (for better or worse) in a realistic manner. Make a list of how your life today would be different if one or two things had changed in the previous day.

83. ANSWER THE SIX UNIVERSAL QUESTIONS

To really understand something, we can ask the six universal questions about it. The six universal questions are: who, what, where, when, why, and how. By answering these six questions when thinking of any single thing, you ensure you're covering all areas for understanding it more fully:

- Who is this for and who does it impact?
- What is it, what could it be, what is it not?
- Where is it, where could it be?
- When did this get created, when will it cease to matter?
- Why does it matter?
- How did it get here?

YOUR CHALLENGE: Write down and answer six universal questions (and any related questions, like the ones written above) about a challenge in your life. Have a friend answer the same questions and see where your answers are similar and where they are not.

84. PLAY DESCRIPTIVE CHARADES

One of the most powerful ways of describing something to someone else is by how it looks. Trying to describe or understand an object simply by how it looks uses the parts of your brain linked to imagination and problem solving: connecting one idea (like the color of the thing) to another (like the texture of the thing) in order to create a solid understanding. This method helps you conjure an image in your mind's eye that's more vivid and thorough. For example: a cloud can be a cloud, or it can be a soft ball of white-colored fur, slowly floating in a pool of blue water up in the sky.

YOUR CHALLENGE:

This challenge requires friends or family members to play along. Using a sheet of paper or other writing mechanism, everyone separately thinks up and writes down a clear description of a unique and specific object (a person, place, or thing). Everyone must write down their description to ensure nobody tries making up additional details on the next step. Once everyone has written their description, one by one everyone takes turns reading the description they've written to see who can guess what's being described quickest.

85. LAUGH OUT LOUD

Great news: it turns out that those funny YouTube videos you get sucked into watching could help your creativity. Research from the University of Western Ontario found that watching a humorous video increased "cognitive flexibility" in participants. Meaning: if you watch something funny that can put you into a positive mood, you're more likely to have what scientists and psychologists refer to as "a broad mental horizon," which means you'll be more optimistic about possibilities. The trick, you might find, is how to *stop* yourself from continuing to watch videos once you've started.

YOUR CHALLENGE: Take a 10-minute break to look up some funny videos online or to check if there's anything funny on TV. Share with others the video that makes you laugh loudest.

86. WRITE AN EVERYDAY RECIPE

It's easy to look at something for exactly what it is. What requires thinking is looking at that same thing as a collection of smaller pieces. A car is easy to define as "a car," but it's also plastic, metal, screws, rubber, lights, paint, hinges, and much more. To make the car move, a series of machinery has to work together. By thinking of an object in terms of what makes it what it is and what makes it perform its task, we give ourselves a keener eye from which to view the world around us. Something you might take for granted—like your car starting every morning—actually requires a huge number of smaller parts to work correctly. An appreciation for the enormity of that challenge can lead you to insights you might be missing.

YOUR CHALLENGE: Create a "recipe" for something you interact with daily, whether it's a car, a dish, a machine, a building, or even a person in your life. Get as descriptive as possible and write down the ingredients and recipe, step by step, as if it were part of a cookbook.

87. CREATE AN IDEA SPRINGBOARD

Psychologists George M. Prince and William J.J. Gordon developed a unique way of brainstorming called "springboarding." The idea is to use irrational ideas as "springboards" for more logical thoughts. To use springboarding, you write down a number of extreme ideas beginning with "I wish . . ." or "How to . . ." then find ways to turn those extreme ideas into realistic and feasible ones. For example: "I wish I could fly." Of course I can fly, in an airplane, by skydiving, or hang-gliding. I can take that springboard further and say: "I wish I could fly without any of the typical means of flight." This springboard leads me to think of setting a desktop fan in front of my face while I close my eyes and simply imagine myself flying over valleys of the world. I'd look silly, but at least I'd be flying. This method works by stretching your thinking outside the realm of realistic possibilities—into absurdity and irrelevance—then rubber-banding yourself back to reality in order to develop the ideas.

YOUR CHALLENGE:

Write down something you dream of doing. Beneath that statement, quickly write down any ideas that seem absurd, illogical, or far-fetched on how you can achieve the dream. When you can't think of any more zany ideas, look back through the list and pick one or two ideas you can outline in more realistic ways.

88. CONNECT BEHAVIORS TO THEIR EMOTIONS

Inventor and psychologist William J.J. Gordon once wrote, "Creative output increases when people become aware of the psychological processes that control their behavior." In other words: to be more creative, you need to be aware of what drives you to act or think in certain ways. One such driver is your emotions, which are easy to neglect despite their ability to impact your thinking. When you capture an emotion and think about what it causes you to do, you can use those insights to drive creative thinking in the future.

YOUR CHALLENGE: Write a list of three emotions you felt yesterday or today, one emotion per line. Next to each emotion, write something specific you did while feeling that emotion. Finally, next to the thing you did, write something that came just before it. Now, read each line backwards to see how certain events affect your emotion and thinking.

89. CREATE A BLACKOUT POEM

Artist and writer Austin Kleon is known for taking a big, black marker to newspaper articles and blacking out all of the words on the page except a select few. The result is a funny-looking, but deeply simplistic and moving, poem made up from the words Kleon didn't cover. The constraint of creating something like a poem from an existing set of words you see on a page (like that of a newspaper article) can be remarkably powerful for thinking creatively. The technique requires you to see what's already there and imagine how it can be altered to present a different message.

YOUR CHALLENGE: Take a note from Kleon's work to create your own blackout poem. Find something you can draw on: a newspaper or magazine article, a page from a book, or even something you've written yourself. Try to make a poem by blacking out all of the words you want to exclude, leaving visible only the words you want as part of your poem.

 EMERGENT

90. CHANGE ENVIRONMENTS

Your environment has a greater impact on your thoughts than you may realize. An artist who likes working in a quiet studio is likely to have the focus and privacy to explore ideas, where that same artist might struggle to focus if she tried painting on a busy street corner. Surround yourself with inspiration or ideas that can inspire you, and you're much more likely to find yourself coming up with creative ideas than if you were to spend all of your time in an environment void of creative material. To spark new inspiration in yourself, change your environment and pay attention to how it makes you feel.

YOUR CHALLENGE: Go to a new environment, one where you're likely to run into inspirational things, and create a list of everything that inspires you there. Some examples would be a museum with contemporary works, a library filled with elaborate book covers, a school campus where students openly discuss ideas, or a local cafe where local artists display art or perform it.

91. OBSERVE SOMETHING NEW

Everything in our minds—our opinions, routines, and ideas—is a result of our experiences. The way we view the world is shaped entirely by what we do, hear, taste, feel, see, and otherwise experience. When we encounter something new, we try to make sense of that new experience by comparing it to what we already know. This mental comparison is what leads us to have a wider understanding of the world and what's possible within it. Therefore, to expand your creativity, you need to expand your experiences and observe something new.

YOUR CHALLENGE: Find five new things to observe in the next 5 minutes. It can be anything from a 30-second video, a new corner of a building you've never been in, or a dance move you make up and perform in front of the mirror for the sake of seeing something new.

92. FINISH AN INCOMPLETE DOODLE

It's easy to look at a scribbled mark on paper and see it as nothing more than a mark. The same goes for everything we encounter in life: the roads, buildings, friendly faces, and so on. They all represent exactly what we expect them to be and little more. To think creatively, you must find new ways to see things differently, to imagine things not as they are but as they could be. Albert Einstein once famously quipped, "Creativity is seeing what everyone else has seen, and thinking what no one else has thought." To do this, you need to look long enough at something as simple as a mark on paper to see what it could evolve into.

YOUR CHALLENGE: Using a sheet of paper and a pencil or the space here, quickly scribble a line on the paper. (It can be a straight line or a wiggly one, big or small, whatever you feel like in the moment.) Once the mark is made, spend the next 5 minutes turning it into a complete picture that anyone seeing would understand. Share what you draw and see if others can accurately guess what it is you've imagined.

93. ACT OUT A DAYDREAM

For many people, daydreaming comes and goes in a snap. But a surprising thing happens when you allow your daydream to play out longer, in your real life. In 2009, neuroscientists showed that purposeful daydreaming can not only help solve problems, but it also opens our minds to the type of thinking that leads to creative insights. Author and innovation expert Matthew E. May has written on this very thing, saying, "It's when our minds wander that our brains do their best work . . . It's dedicated daydreaming—purposeful mind wandering—that yields productive creativity."

YOUR CHALLENGE: Daydream for a moment that you have just received the best news in the world, whatever that may mean for you. Starting now, act as if that news were real and true. How would you act differently? How does acting that way impact your day?

94. IMAGIPLAIN SOMETHING

Have you ever tried to explain something and have someone understand what it was you were describing? By explaining the details of something—rather than outright saying what it is—you are forced to think of even the most minute details of that thing in order to create a vivid image of it in the mind. This presents a unique opportunity to really think deeply about the thing you're trying to describe, noting details you usually glance over or don't fully consider. I call this technique "imagiplaining," or imagined explaining. Trying to describe a pineapple, for example, describing nothing but how the fruit looks can be a laborious (and even humorous) challenge.

YOUR CHALLENGE: This challenge needs to be done with a friend, coworker, or family member. Each of you takes turns using your imaginations to describe—in detail—the appearance of a single object. The other person tries to guess what is being described as quickly as possible. The first person to stump the other, despite giving a detailed description of the thing, wins.

95. BATHROOM THINK

Author and entrepreneur Elizabeth Grace Saunders once said, "If you don't make a conscious choice for rest, you will find yourself always filling your time by ticking off items . . ." It can be hard to find any time for rest, let alone privacy, in today's troubled and hectic world, though. Fortunately, there is a culturally driven opportunity to "get away from it all" in most environments: the bathroom. Bathrooms are often the most personal and quiet places you can be in, for good reasons (of course). Taking a break to get away from distractions, responsibilities, and even your own thinking, can give you a much-needed mental boost that can help get your mind into a more creative state.

YOUR CHALLENGE: Find the nearest bathroom, sit down, and give your brain a break for a few minutes (no using a phone or book while you're in there!). Use the private space as an opportunity to relax as best as possible and sit with your idle thoughts.

96. COPY SOMEONE ELSE'S IDEA

Famous film director Jean-Luc Godard once said, "It's not where you take things from, it's where you take them to." Godard was right, since everything in life is built from or inspired by something else that came before it. To be creative, you should look at ways to copy someone else's idea and make it your own. Writer and performer John Cleese wrote about this very point in his autobiography *So, Anyway . . .* where he wrote: "Steal. Steal an idea that you know is good, and try to reproduce it in a setting that you know and understand. It will become sufficiently different from the original because *you* are writing it, and by basing it on something good, you will be learning some of the rules . . . as you go along." Take his advice, and you might just create something new and amazing from someone else's starting point.

YOUR CHALLENGE:

Find one great work you admire that you can copy (a painting, a poem, a photograph, a business idea, a song, anything). Copy the idea and make it into your own, however you can, today. Share what you create.

97. ASK WITHOUT ASKING

We rarely need to think deeply about the words we use every day in conversation. The result is that we become effective communicators, but boring ones. Exploring how to communicate without using the words you usually use forces you to think of common tasks and questions in new ways. If you had to communicate without explicitly saying what you're trying to say, new perspectives on the same old topics start to emerge. For example: asking for a glass of water becomes "looking for something to wet your tongue." Trying to find the bathroom becomes "wanting to discover a private place to take care of nature's business."

YOUR CHALLENGE: Go to a public place—a shopping center, school, or workplace—and ask three separate people questions without explicitly saying what you're asking. Have a friend play the same challenge and see who can get an answer for what they're asking (without straightforwardly asking it) faster.

98. SHARPEN-EXPAND YOUR FOCUS

There are many small, even microscopic, moving parts to everything around us. We often don't take the time to think about how one small movement within a thing affects the larger part we see. For example: the turning of a screw, tightening against wood grain. How that wood strains from being pulled, strengthening the shape. By focusing on one small attribute of movement, and imagining how that small part affects the larger whole (and how that larger part affects other things, on and on), you can gain new perspectives on even the most familiar things.

YOUR CHALLENGE:

Look up and, noting the first thing you see, imagine how even the smallest part of that object affects much more than the object itself. Think of the smallest element all the way to the biggest, imagining how one affects the other, unseen.

99. DRAW TO MIX AND MATCH PARTS

Steve Jobs once exclaimed, "Creativity is just connecting things," and to some degree, he was right. By looking at how the parts of one thing combine with another, you not only make it easy to imagine what something new would look like, you also increase the likelihood that you'll stumble onto new ways of using or looking at the existing ideas that were combined. For example: imagining what a computer would look like as a phone, what a music player would look like without any physical buttons, or a laptop as thin as just a few sheets of paper stacked together. Mixing and matching parts of ideas can lead to worthwhile new ideas.

YOUR CHALLENGE: Imagine what you could create by combining parts of three or more things near you now, doodling at least nine possibilities of the results on a sheet of paper or in the space here. Combine only the parts you can see, illustrating any actions or uses you imagine for the objects as well.

 EMERGENT

100. TAKE A SHOWER

Have you ever found yourself feeling as though you're wasting time because you were doing something not particularly interesting? Research indicates that those moments of "downtime" are crucial for thinking creatively, because they allow our minds to go over deep questions and modes of thinking without the constant interruption of conversations, notifications, advertisements, and so on. One such moment of downtime that is prized by artists, musicians, and researchers alike: taking a shower.

YOUR CHALLENGE: If possible, stop whatever you're doing right now and go hop in the shower. If you have to schedule it for later, do so. The break away from your regular thinking can give you just what you need to start feeling energized and creative.

101. INVITE AN IMAGINARY PERSON OVER

Placing yourself into imaginary situations is a great way to break apart your regular thinking patterns. Even better: imagine placing something (or someone) else into your current situation. By imagining someone else with you now, you gain an imaginary outside perspective on yourself. That added perspective may be imaginary, but by thinking of the different ways other people may view you, you frame yourself in a way that requires an original point of view.

YOUR CHALLENGE: Imagine what your dentist, doctor, favorite barista, or teacher would say if he or she were with you right now. Think about how your behavior would change as a result of that person being present, and act the situation out as if it were real.

102. EXPLORE WHAT YOU ALREADY KNOW

Creativity expert Michael Michalko has a great way of describing how the brain works. He says it's like a bowl of ice cream, and when you pour water over it, the water creates shallow paths in the ice cream. If you keep pouring water over the ice cream, some of the water flows to create new paths, but the majority of it will flow down the existing paths. You'll also have ruined a perfectly good bowl of ice cream. This metaphor describes how our brains interpret information, constantly trying to place it in existing pathways of thinking. To be creative, Michalko explains, you must find ways to break away from your existing paths for thinking and re-evaluate what you think you already know.

YOUR CHALLENGE: Create a list of fifty unique questions about something you think you know a lot about. For example: I use pens to write every day. My fifty questions would include: Why is black the primary color used in pens? Is there an "ideal" handle length for a pen to be? Who invented the pen anyway? Challenge a friend to come up with his own list and see who asks the most surprising question.

103. WRITE AN IMAGINED INTERVIEW

Conversations are directional, in that they have a clear start and end. Everything that comes in the middle of a conversation is merely the evolution of the start in order to reach the end. We can use the common language associated with a conversation (or, in this case, an imaginary interview) to look at things from a surprisingly progressive, and even lateral, perspective. Plus, because the interview is imaginary, you get to see two sides of whatever you decide to write about.

YOUR CHALLENGE: Write an imaginary interview with someone who inspires you. Ask and answer at least ten unique questions to that person within your imaginary interview.

104. PICTURE PAREIDOLIA

Pareidolia is a psychological illusion that means seeing things that aren't really there, like looking at a few marks on a wall and seeing a face, or looking at a cloud and seeing an animal. Research shows that our ability to see things that aren't really there (like a face where there is none) is the result of evolution. Evolutionary advantage aside, pareidolia is a great way to induce imaginative thinking by exposing yourself to new ways of looking at boring or otherwise familiar things we might encounter on a regular basis.

YOUR CHALLENGE:

Grab a camera or something to draw with and go on a hunt for pareidolia, capturing (by taking a picture or doodling) anything you see that resembles a face, animal, or other object, without actually being that object.

105. TUNE IN TO MOZART

In 1993, research led by Professor Frances Rauscher of the University of Wisconsin Oshkosh indicated that listening to music by Mozart has a profoundly surprising impact on thinking ability. The researchers concluded that listening to the works of Mozart (specifically his sonata K448) for 10 minutes led to an increase in spatial reasoning skills. In 2001, J.S. Jenkins of the University of Illinois Medical Center reaffirmed the initial research: Listening to Mozart has a powerful impact on your ability to think creatively.

YOUR CHALLENGE: Listen to the work of Mozart today. Make notes on how listening to the music makes you feel, and whether you see a difference in your ability to think creatively, or not, as a result.

106. CONNECT TO A FAVORITE STORY

Our brains are constantly connecting ideas together in order to shape new ideas, solve problems, and make sense of the world around us. Anything you can add to the mishmash of ideas happening in your head allows you to gain new perspectives and create new understandings. One of the best ways to build new connections is through the stories others tell, from their unique perspectives. Actively listening to a story helps you appreciate other people's perspectives on what's important to share, the words they use, and the manner in which they convey what's happening.

YOUR CHALLENGE: Get someone today to tell you one of her favorite life stories that relates to something happening in your own life right now. Topics could range from what you ate for breakfast to a problem you are currently experiencing.

107. CREATE NEW FALSE BELIEFS

Researchers at the University of Auckland found a connection between understanding false beliefs (the beliefs we have that might not reflect reality) and the ability to think divergently. This should come as no surprise: The things we believe about the world aren't always based on fact—our egos and personal biases tend to get in the way of what's really true. This means you can stir up ideas by creating stories or made-up facts, then thinking of what changes would make those false beliefs true.

YOUR CHALLENGE: Come up with the most bizarre yet believable fact about something you encounter every day. Then, try to get someone to believe your "fact." Here is an idea: The bathtub was originally invented for astronauts to sleep in during flight. Or: the first telephone was made of concrete to keep it from getting lost.

108. MAKE A REPLACEMENT POEM

We can take apart anything we experience to define what caused it and the result. A song we hear can be broken down into melodies, notes, and rhythms. The same goes for artistic works, movies, dances, and writing. By looking at each individual piece of something, and evaluating what would happen if you replaced any of them, you uncover the value of the smaller piece and the place it has within the whole.

YOUR CHALLENGE: Quickly find or think of a saying or quote, or a short poem, you can use for reference in this challenge. Rewrite whatever you've found by keeping the same first and last words, but replacing each word in between them to create an entirely new poem.

109. NARROW YOUR VISION

In the 1920s, the painter Piet Mondrian looked at the constraints of painting—the paintbrush, the canvas, and the colors—and decided to add even more constraints. He would only paint using solid, bold colors, using only straight lines and 90-degree angles. The result was a new style of painting: Neo-Plasticism. Visual constraints force us to focus on a small area of what we see or imagine, to the point where we are driven to think of how the constraints can be used for generating original ideas, like Mondrian's approach to painting.

YOUR CHALLENGE: Constrain how you look at the world for the next 10 minutes. Look only through your hands (closed in the shape of two circles, like binoculars), cut holes in a sheet of paper to look through, squint, or use some other means of narrowing what you see.

 EMERGENT

110. CREATE A MIND SCULPTURE

Ian Robertson, psychology professor at the Trinity College in Dublin, studied the effects of visualization—imagining yourself in a situation or behaving in a certain way—and found that spending just 15 minutes visualizing creates lasting neurological changes within the brain. Robertson came up with a method for harnessing visualization, called "Mind Sculpture." Rather than simply imagining the visuals associated with a desired outcome, participants should focus on seeing as well as hearing, smelling, touching, and tasting their ideal situation. Adding the dimension of your five senses makes your visualization much more real and thus more likely to build new neurological pathways.

YOUR CHALLENGE: Set a timer for 15 minutes and find a comfortable place to sit and relax. Close your eyes after the timer starts and imagine yourself being more creative, whatever that means for you. Don't simply imagine what you see in that situation, but think about what you hear and smell, what you feel with your hands, and what you taste.

111. DESCRIBE THE INDESCRIBABLE

Actor and writer John Cleese once famously quipped, "When you're being creative, nothing is wrong." Unlike our regular modes of thinking, creative thinking requires us to explore possibilities that may not have a right or wrong answer. While our default mode of thinking is to converge on ideas as a way of understanding them (by comparing one thing to another), creative thinking requires that we converge ideas without sticking to pre-made assumptions. Any attempt to describe something indescribable would therefore need creativity behind it.

YOUR CHALLENGE:

Without thinking about it too hard, answer the following questions out loud, no matter where you are now:

1. What does the color red smell like?
2. How many breaths does it take to box up this sentence?
3. Who is responsible for painting rain?

112. TAKE AN OPPOSITE DAY

To find a unique perspective, we can look to the opposite of how we're used to thinking (or behaving). When we look at a situation from an opposite perspective, we uncover areas of thinking that would otherwise lie hidden behind our assumptions or default behaviors. Taking an opposite day, or doing the opposite of what you usually do, can help to unlock those hidden insights. Rather than trying to be creative, for example, you could try not being creative at all. You might wind up with creative insights as a result.

YOUR CHALLENGE: Starting now, do everything as though it were the opposite of what you would normally or ideally do. If you would usually drive somewhere, stay exactly where you are. If you would spend time reading, spend time writing. Do the opposite of what you intend to do, for as long as you can.

113. CATCH A MOVIE ENDING

Most movies work in a fairly standard format: A problem leads to a pursuit, which leads to a climax, which leads to a resolution. If you miss one part of the movie, you're left to your imagination to piece together what could have happened or will happen next. This helps explain why movies with cliff-hangers leave us feeling so energized. It also explains why catching only the beginning or ending of a movie can fire up your imagination.

YOUR CHALLENGE: Find a movie you haven't seen before or haven't watched in a very long time. Fast-forward to the last 10 minutes of the film and watch from there. No matter how badly you want to watch more of the film, restrict yourself to the ending and let your imagination go wild with what led to it.

114. DRAW YOUR THOUGHT BUBBLE

When you think about how you think (the words and language, that is), what does it look like to you? Trying to imagine what thoughts *look like* in the brain is a mystery that has baffled scientists and artists for centuries. Trying to imagine thoughts as visible, tangible things, gives them the traits of things you can more easily manipulate and share. By drawing your thoughts as they might actually appear, you give them that same mutability (or ability to be altered).

YOUR CHALLENGE:

Take 10 or more minutes to draw yourself and a speech bubble coming from your head with any and all thoughts you have in a regular day in it.

115. MAKE A POSTCARD

Traditional postcards are small photographs—just slightly larger than the size of a modern-day cell phone—that you can write on the back of and then mail to someone. Because postcards are small in size, they require you to think a lot harder about what you want to write than, say, a normal letter. In addition to the limited size, the photograph on the postcard should reflect whatever it is you write on it as well. These constraints act as sparks for thinking creatively about a vacation . . . or a problem you're currently tackling.

YOUR CHALLENGE: Find a postcard you can use in a store, or print your own photograph, to make a postcard you can send to a friend (use e-mail if you want). Think about the photo you want to use, then write in only a few sentences to go alongside it.

116. REVERSE YOUR DAY

Time runs forward; there's no other way for it to run. However, with a little imagination, you can make time go in any direction you want, from any point in the past or future. So, while you're used to seeing time move in one direction, imagining it running in any other direction can help you think in unique and surprisingly imaginative ways. This is a great technique for generating creative ideas or solving problems that require a more imaginative solution.

YOUR CHALLENGE: Take a few minutes to imagine yourself in an ideal situation in the near future. Write down everything that will happen in that future and how you got from where you are today to that point, writing the steps backwards in time.

117. ACT OUT DISSIMILAR SITUATIONS

In order to look at your thoughts in new and surprising ways (so you can see things uniquely and to think creatively), you need look no further than your imagination. By imagining yourself in a different setting than you are currently in, or by imagining the same setting but with a different task or goal, you lead yourself to inevitably notice things in new ways because your new, imagined situation forces you to. Sometimes the spark your imagination needs to get going is encountering something surprisingly uncommon, like putting something somewhere it doesn't belong and imagining what would happen as a result.

YOUR CHALLENGE: Act as if you are exactly where you are now, but your objective has suddenly changed. Now you're not simply reading a book, you're in the middle of playing a sport, performing a play, directing a movie, or at a zoo.

118. MAKE A RUBE GOLDBERG MACHINE

Named after the cartoonist and inventor, a Rube Goldberg machine is any complex setup that uses a chain reaction to accomplish a simple task. These types of "machines" make the lateral and linear connections between objects obvious. For example: imagine knocking over a shoe, which pushes a rubber ball toward a glass of water, which then spills over and pushes a miniature paper sailboat into a toy, which then falls off of a table, pulling a string along with it, which turns on a light switch in your bedroom. A chain of events like this can inspire you to see inevitable cause-and-effect relationships in your work or life.

YOUR CHALLENGE: Create a Rube Goldberg machine of your own using any materials you can. It doesn't matter what the machine you make does, only that it uses a lot of steps to do something simple. Invite a friend to create the machine with you to see if she can add any twists.

 AESTHETIC

119. SOLVE THIS CHALLENGE

Beau Lotto is an astirt who dtceedias his lfie to snohwig jsut how cveirtae our mnids can be. Lotto uess inluslios and scnicee to detamsntroe how our mndis are nltralauy dirven to flil in the blnkas and mkae ssnee of tinhgs, eevn tnghis lkie sacrlembd wodrs. Reesrcah form Cardmibge Uesivinrty has shwon taht Lotto is rghit: Eevn wehn the leettrs of wdros are meixd up, we can siltl uedtnasnrd waht's wetrtin.

YOUR CHALLENGE: Unscramble the words above to turn the paragraph from one made up of seemingly gibberish to one of real words. Hint: the words are already there, you just need to look closely to unscramble them.

120. ESCAPE YOUR PRESSURES

Author and actor John Cleese had it right when he said, "You can't become playful, and therefore creative, if you're under your usual pressures." Even the smallest stress created from pressure can be enough to dampen your ability to think creatively and explore possibilities. Yet who isn't exposed to a lot of stress in everyday life? You can't avoid it entirely, but you can learn to relieve it for a moment. In order to think more freely, you must find temporary escape from whatever pressures you feel.

YOUR CHALLENGE: Think about what pressures are weighing down on you right now, from annoyances and deadlines to family concerns or fears of failure. Whatever the pressure is, identify its opposite (being away from the annoyance, not having a deadline, etc.). Spend the next 10 or more minutes pursuing that opposite.

121. CONNECT RANDOM THINGS

Some of the best ideas come as a result of connecting random things, like peanut butter and chocolate. By making seemingly unrelated connections like that, you bring to light everything the different parts have in common or ways they could work together that you might otherwise take for granted or not notice. How the sweet can complement the sour, bad ideas can inspire good ones, and heavy things can weigh down lighter things.

YOUR CHALLENGE: Gather as many random things around you as you can right now. Find a way to combine them in wacky, but realistic, ways to create something new. Challenge a friend to do the same and see who can come up with the most original way of connecting the things together.

122. FIND TEN WAYS TO DO SOMETHING IMPOSSIBLE

The word "impossible" simply means unreasonable. To think creatively is to use your imagination in sometimes unreasonable ways: to travel through time, to become a super version of yourself, or to see things that are invisible. But creativity isn't only about imagining the impossible; it's about finding ways to connect the impossible things with the possible ones. This challenge will encourage you to link the two and make the impossible, possible.

YOUR CHALLENGE: List ten imaginative ways to do something impossible. For example: to travel the entire world by only spending $100, you could get a job as a flight attendant, you could hitchhike, or just use Google Earth online to "virtually" travel the world and spend the $100 on something else.

123. WRITE A SERIES OF "PO"

Po stands for Provocative Operation. Author and creativity expert Edward de Bono came up with po in an attempt to help move thinking forward, even when we feel mentally stuck or uninspired. Essentially, po means moving your ideas forward no matter how silly, dumb, absurd, poorly defined, or otherwise impractical they seem to you. Forcing your mind to consider options no matter how far-fetched or illogical they seem results in a pattern of thinking that leads from impossibility to realistically feasible. How? By tapping into your brain's natural tendency to solve problems. An example would be first to think about something you want to do (a goal in your life, for example) then use a po to decide what action to take. "Find the simplest way to start," could be an example po. So could: "Ask a stranger what to do." The point of po is to ask questions that will get you moving on an idea no matter what.

YOUR CHALLENGE:

Think of something that could be classified as "impossible." Then come up with a list of ten po on how to make that impossibility into something possible. Circle the one that seems most realistic, then create ten additional po for that po.

 AESTHETIC

124. DOODLE YOUR OUTLINE

Our minds process and record a lot of visual information, more than we often realize. While our eyes are capturing roughly 10 million different signals every second, only a fraction of what we see ever makes it to our conscious brain. According to neuroscientists, what we think we see is only made up of about 10 percent of what is really in front of us. The rest of what we "see" is made up in our brains based on our other senses, memories, and even our imaginations. To harness the other 90 percent of subconscious visual information your brain has stored in it—in order to think more imaginatively or to gain creative insights—requires a keen focus or a captivating challenge.

YOUR CHALLENGE: Draw a basic outline of a person on a sheet of paper or in the space here, then doodle how you think you look within the outline. Doodle as many details about your appearance that you can remember, then show the drawing to someone and have him guess who it is (if he guesses you correctly, congratulations).

125. IGNORE TIME

Taking a break from the worries and anxieties of life can be refreshing, but doing so can also help you feel empowered. Research like that of Sandra L. Bloom from Drexel University School of Public Health shows that giving yourself a way to temporarily remove negative stressors from your life has tremendous benefits for your health and mind. One such way to break away from reality for a bit: ignore time. Doing so can calm your mind, alleviate stress, and make you think about what you're spending your time on every day. Initially, ignoring time may seem more stressful (what if you miss a meeting?), but you can train yourself to find slots during your day to do so. You'll find yourself approaching the concept of time in ways that are undoubtedly more open and flexible than you're usually used to.

YOUR CHALLENGE:

Act as though time has suddenly stopped for you (and only you). Since you don't have to worry about clocks moving forward, deadlines, or aging, what will you do to pass the "time"? Act out this scenario for as long as you can get away with it.

126. WRITE USING MALAPROPISMS

A malapropism is the use of an incorrect word mistakenly in place of another, similar sounding one. For example: angel instead of angle, accept instead of except, or particle instead of article. Without knowing it, you may have used malapropisms when writing or speaking in your own life. They're not as uncommon as many of us would like them to be. Because the words are similar in how they sound and appear, it's easy to mistake one for the other. What's fun is trying to come up with malapropisms on your own, in an attempt to think deeply about what each word means and how mixing them up causes unintentional (and often humorous) results.

YOUR CHALLENGE: Using the three examples above (angel, accept, and particle), come up with three sentences that would be humorous when the malapropism is used in place of the correct word. For example: "We measured all the angels of the triangle, but they wouldn't add up!"

127. MAKE SOUND-BASED NAMES

Since the time of ancient Greece, philosophers have debated what language is and where it stems from (emotions or logical thought). If you've ever wondered why we call things by a certain name (like why cars are called "cars"), you're part of that discussion. You can also understand language and the names of things by exploring imaginative alternatives. For example: coming up with a new name for something, based on a sound, is where things get really interesting.

YOUR CHALLENGE: Look around you and note the first thing you see. Think of a sound that could represent that thing, then use the sound to come up with a new name for the object. Try it for several of the things around you now. As an example: a towel sounds like "Fffuuhhhssshhuu" to me, so my new name for a towel would be Fuhsh.

128. DISPROVE THE OBVIOUS

When we assume things are obvious (because we're overly familiar with them or because we've accepted them as being the way they are simply because that's the way they should be), we miss a chance to fully understand those things or why they matter. By questioning anything that "goes without saying," you can expand your knowledge around exactly why that may be the case. Such a task is easier said than done, of course, since obvious things (like "what goes up, must come down") are engrained in us throughout our entire lives, simply because it's easy to accept the thing as it is rather than to question it and explore it. But pushing yourself to disprove something you accept as truth is a great exercise in pushing the creative envelope.

YOUR CHALLENGE:

Take something that is obvious and question it by taking an opposite view or thinking about what would make it false. Try to effectively convince someone that the obvious thing is false by using your unique, opposite perspective of it.

 AESTHETIC

129. TWO-HANDED DRAWING

Our brains are wired to favor motor control on certain sides of our bodies over the other. Attempting to use your opposite hand (left hand for right-handed people, right hand for left-handed) to do something you usually do with your dominant hand can therefore be fairly difficult. Thankfully, the struggle of trying to do something with the opposite side of your body is worth it—you'll get a creative boost from it. Specifically, you'll see how both sides of your brain approach something like doodling—one without much thought, the other requiring patience and coordination. For example: if you want to see what your motor controls and mind are doing when you doodle, try drawing a mirrored image using both hands.

YOUR CHALLENGE: Hold a pen or marker in each of your hands and press them into a sheet of paper at the same point. Doodle as you normally would with your dominant hand, but mirror every motion you make with your opposite hand to create a mirror-like image on each side of the page.

130. GIVE YOURSELF AN INSPIRATION FIX

Sometimes we come across something that moves us on a truly deep level, capturing our attention or causing our blood to pump harder than usual. That thing might be a song we hear on the radio, a painting we stumble across at a museum, or an article we read online. When we encounter the right type of inspiration, we feel energized and motivated to see life from the perspective of the person (or persons) that created the inspiration. But how often do you give yourself time to pursue inspiration with the sole intent of being energized by it?

YOUR CHALLENGE: Set a timer for exactly 10 minutes, then do whatever you can to load up on inspiration. Browse the Internet, open your favorite book(s), look around you, call up a friend, or anything else that can help you come face-to-face with something truly inspirational. When you find something that really captures your attention, dedicate an additional 10 minutes to ask yourself why that particular item draws you in so powerfully.

131. SPEAK ONLY IN RHYME

When you speak only in rhyme (for an hour or all the time), your brain might feel like it's turned into slime. But by thinking in this way (for a few minutes or all day), your thoughts will surely turn into an elegant idea buffet. Do your best and nothing else will matter. You'll find that when you do, your thoughts will begin to clatter. You might even secretly be a poet, you just didn't yet know it.

YOUR CHALLENGE:

Today speak only in rhyme for a predetermined amount of time. Invite a friend to do the same and turn this challenge into a game.

 DIVERGENT

132. ACT OUT YOUR OPPOSITE

To open our imaginations to possibilities, we can simply try imagining things as being different than they really are. The act of imagining what would happen if things were different helps lead you to pursue thoughts that you might otherwise never have considered. Thinking about things that never happened (but could have!) requires you to fully engage your imagination. One way of doing just that is to imagine what your current situation would be like (and how you would act) if everything were the opposite of what it really is.

YOUR CHALLENGE: Starting now, act as if your life were the opposite of what it really is. If you're in good health, act as if you were suddenly sick. If you're in a quiet environment, act as if it had suddenly become extremely noisy. If things were the opposite, how would you act differently?

133. WRITE A CAUSE-AND-EFFECT CHAIN

We often don't think of what could happen at any given moment (unless we're daydream inclined), because we often already know what will happen next. Thinking and experiencing the same things day in and day out can leave us feeling comfortable, but it is likely to also make us bored and unimaginative. When you stop to ponder how one small thing can lead to another—a cause and effect—you allow yourself to explore things you normally wouldn't consider. This broad approach to seeing and thinking then exposes your imagination to things you usually may take for granted or fail to notice due to biases in your thinking.

YOUR CHALLENGE: Write a chain of twenty-five events, in the order they would occur, if you were to do something unexpected right now in this moment. Begin with: "If I were to do this . . ." then continue writing what would happen as a result, what would happen from that result, and so on, until you reach twenty-five items.

134. SEEK OUT MAJOR COLORS

You might think you're more observant than you really are. In studies recording how attentive people are to their surroundings and how observant those same people think they are, researchers found that nearly 100 percent of the time, we miss something we thought we were paying attention to. This means we're missing out on seeing inspiration when it might be directly in front of us simply because we're not used to seeing it or because it doesn't align with what we think is right and important about our lives. The only way to know for sure what you miss is to really look closely at what's around you as often as possible.

YOUR CHALLENGE: Find one object near you now that's each of these major colors: red, green, blue, purple, yellow, black, and white. Ask a friend to help you find any of the colors you're struggling to find if you get stuck.

 EMERGENT

135. TUNE IN TO A BEGINNING

To think creatively, we sometimes merely need to fuel our imaginations to ignite our creative fire. Imagination is a core aspect of being able to think differently, so finding a way to empower it can help you to think more creatively. Researchers have shown this to be true, as our brains are naturally drawn to completing puzzles, finishing sentences, and resolving issues we encounter in our lives. By "tuning in" to a beginning, you give your imagination the starting point from which it can run wild and free.

YOUR CHALLENGE: Turn on a random video, open a book or magazine, or start listening to a song, but then stop after only a minute. Let your imagination take over as it tries to explore what can come as a result of the beginning.

136. WORK ON A PROBLEM WITH A FRIEND

The different perspectives each of us has are shaped by the various experiences we encounter in life. For example: what you see and experience in your life is going to be different than what I see and experience, even if we're seeing the same thing at the same time. You can utilize the different perspectives of friends to see things in possibly new light, particularly if what you are getting the different perspective on is something you've had the same view of day in and day out. Something as simple as working on a problem or project with a friend can be all you need to broaden your perspective and think differently, because the way another person approaches the problem is enough to shine a light on the way you think yourself.

YOUR CHALLENGE:

Find a problem you can tackle with a friend and work on it together today or tomorrow (or until the problem or project is completed). Whether the problem is a puzzle, a crossword or sudoku problem, simply planning your day, or building something physical, find time to collaborate.

137. EXPLORE OTHER CULTURES

Through research conducted at Northwestern University, Adam Galinsky found that those who have lived abroad tend to solve problems more creatively than those who haven't. While experiencing everyday mundane activities—like going to the grocery store, riding to school or work, or eating dinner—from the perspective of a different culture, your mind is opened to the possibility that doing things one way or another is never the only way. Thankfully, you don't have to live in another country for an entire summer to get the same benefits of this mental broadening. In one of Galinksy's tests, people who merely watched a 45-minute presentation about life in China improved their creative tests results. So get ready to experience other cultures right from the comfort of your own home.

YOUR CHALLENGE: Spend today or tomorrow exploring another culture by reading about it, watching a presentation or movie about it, cooking food you would get from that part of the world, and otherwise imagining that you're living there for the entire day.

138. DRAW A TIMELINE OF YOUR LIFE

Have you ever stepped back to think about all of the experiences (big and small) that have helped get you to where you are today? By removing yourself from the present and seeing how it connects to your past, you give your imagination the momentum to explore how events impact one another. Removing yourself from your present moment also allows you to take a more broad and ambitious look at what you may have taken for granted: your experiences and how they've shaped your thoughts. To see your experiences as more impactful than they appear when you're first encountering them—and to think from a wider perspective—take an imaginary step back and view a timeline of your life.

YOUR CHALLENGE: Draw a timeline of your life, starting with where you are now and working your way backwards. Highlight the big experiences, but also note smaller experiences you might not have otherwise remembered if you didn't stop to think about them.

139. TWO-MINUTE DOODLE SQUARES

We all have an inner critic within our minds. You know the one: the little voice that tells you when you can't do something or when what you are doing might be dumb, silly, or just bad. That voice gets in the way of creativity by ensuring you don't try anything new, different, or exciting. To think differently, you need to find a way to circumvent that inner critic. One way to do that is by introducing constraints on how you explore your ideas. When you combine more than one constraint (like a time limit, size of the ideas or execution of them, or sheer quantity of ideas) you don't give your inner critic enough time to evaluate what you're doing until after you've completed it. This challenge uses all three methods for circumventing your inner critic in order to explore ideas through doodling in 10 total minutes.

YOUR CHALLENGE: Draw five small squares on a sheet of paper or in the space here, then set a timer for 2 minutes. Doodle in the first square for the first 2 minutes. Once the timer goes off, move on to the second square and doodle in it for 2 minutes. Repeat until each square has been doodled in.

140. OVER-INSPIRE YOUR SUBCONSCIOUS

Your mind can only focus on a certain number of things at a time, but your unconscious brain is actually experiencing a lot more than you consciously realize. To feel creatively inspired, you can attempt to overwhelm your subconscious with inspiration that can then bubble up into your consciousness naturally. Think of this like sitting in a crowded and loud room while trying to hear every conversation, and still being able to hear your name called from the opposite side of the room. While your consciousness is distracted, trying to filter out everything going on around you, your subconscious is capturing everything that might help spark new ideas or otherwise be important for you.

YOUR CHALLENGE: Find a way to overwhelm your senses with possible inspiration for at least 10 minutes today. Capture all of the ideas that come to you during that time by writing them down, doodling, or doing a voice recording.

141. TEACH YOURSELF TO READ UPSIDE DOWN

Leonardo da Vinci taught himself to write cursive backwards, so the only way to read his private journals was by viewing them in a mirror. Apart from the added privacy of writing cursive backwards—which would make it incredibly difficult for the average person to read whatever you write—changing how you read or write allows you to see and think of what you're writing from a unique perspective. Suddenly things that were common (like writing the word "the") become perplexing, because you're doing them differently than how you're used to. The challenge of doing anything backwards or upside down can be difficult, but it's only difficult because it's not what you're used to. That's what makes them valuable to try in the first place.

YOUR CHALLENGE: Find something you can physically hold and read, then turn it upside down. Read it and re-read it until you can easily read the upside-down words without struggling to figure out what they are. Challenge a friend to read the same message upside down.

142. WRITE A NOTE FROM YOUR SHOES

Changing your perspective to that of another person is effective for invoking creative thinking, because the different perspective will be one you aren't used to. Trying to change your mindset to the perspective of an everyday, inanimate object can be equally insightful, albeit somewhat harder to do. By trying to look at the world from the perspective of, say, a pair of running shoes, your imagination begins to think in dramatic terms of what the world might be like from such a drastically unique perspective. This approach to altering your perspective makes you more likely to notice and think about things you wouldn't normally notice or think about. Things like what the underside of a table looks like, what it might be like having to smell feet all day, or how socks are like blankets for your feet.

YOUR CHALLENGE:

Write a note to yourself as though it were written by your shoes. What would your feet say about how they spend their time? "It feels like we've been walking all our lives but never really going anywhere."

143. CONNECT A BEGINNING TO AN ENDING

If you're given a box of puzzle pieces without any picture of what the completed puzzle would look like, you're likely to struggle putting it together. It's only when we have the pieces of the puzzle and a picture or idea of what the final puzzle will look like that you can begin to put pieces where they need to go. The same is true of imaginary scenarios: If you have a beginning and an ending in mind, you can more easily come up with ways to bridge the two together in creative ways, spurring original thinking as a result. Given a start and end, your imagination has everything it needs to make a successful creative solution to bridging the two.

YOUR CHALLENGE:

Open a different book than this one and read the first sentence on the first page. Then skip to the last page and read the last sentence on it. Using your imagination, write down all of the possible ways you can think of that connect the first sentence to the last one, whether they're accurate for that book or not.

144. FINGER-PAINT YOUR EMOTIONS

Research has shown that as far back as 13,000 years ago, people would paint on cave walls using nothing but their fingers and crude paint-like substances. Finger painting today remains a unique way of communicating through broad-stroked, abstract symbols and colors. Because of the way finger painting connects your mind, motor skills, imagination, and other sensory functions, it works effectively as an easier way to invoke creative thinking than other forms of painting or drawing. And because painting any details with fingers covered in paint isn't necessarily easy, the quality of the artwork matters less, which makes you more likely to enjoy the process of creating it. That's why children often enjoy finger painting—they can appreciate the process for what it is and let their creativity lead the way.

YOUR CHALLENGE: Create a finger-painting masterpiece that represents how you feel today. Use colors and shapes that reflect whatever you're feeling here and now. Invite a friend to make one as well and compare paintings afterward.

145. LISTEN TO SOMEONE ELSE

It can be hard to break free of our individual perspectives in life when we're so used to thinking and seeing things from the perspective of our own heads. One method for getting outside of our mental box in order to experience new perspectives is through empathy. By listening to others talk about what's going on in their lives, you temporarily step outside of your own head to see the world from a new perspective. This new perspective (from a friend or acquaintance) can help expose a thinking pattern you didn't know you had, or spark inspiration on how to think differently yourself based on the things you hear someone else talk about. The goal isn't for you to talk about your perspective, but to get the person talking from his or her perspective.

YOUR CHALLENGE: Find someone who has a few minutes to talk, then ask four to five deep-thinking questions while listening intently to the answers. Example questions might be: "What's most important to you right now?" or "Whom are you thinking of and why them?" or "Where would you want to wake up if you could wake up anywhere tomorrow?"

146. WRITE ABOUT AN ABSURD EXPERIENCE

Your brain always tries to make sense of experiences, even when those experiences don't make any logical sense. In one study conducted by Travis Proulx and Steven J. Heine of the University of California, Santa Barbara, people who read an absurd short story before working on a creative thinking task ended up performing better than those who hadn't read the story beforehand. Scientists showed that the absurdity of the story helped to switch participants' minds into a pattern-solving mode that carried over to the task after reading it. You can use this research to invoke the creative pattern-solving and problem-resolving modes in your own brain.

YOUR CHALLENGE: Write one to two pages of an absurd, imaginary experience. The more absurd and random the experience sounds, the more likely you are to benefit from coming up with it and having your brain try to make sense of it.

147. HELP SOMEONE TO THINK DIFFERENTLY

Social psychologists have come up with a theory of thinking that promotes creativity called "construal level theory," or CLT. The theory states that the more removed or far away we perceive something to be from us (even imaginary), the more likely we are to think of it in abstract and therefore creative ways. Because we aren't able to see the visible details of the distant thing, we're inclined to think about it in more broad and open-ended ways. To take advantage of this theory, you can look to help someone else think differently. In doing so, you're likely to discover ways to be more creative yourself, because the task of being more creative is removed from yourself.

YOUR CHALLENGE: Come up with a way to help someone else—a stranger or a friend—to think differently, if only for a brief moment. You can accomplish this challenge by asking the person a surprising question, tasking him with drawing using his opposite hand, or prompting him to complete one of the other challenges within this book.

148. EXPLORE WHAT'S COME BEFORE

We often get stuck on problems or in pursuing our dreams because we doubt ourselves or lose focus on our intention. Thankfully for almost any problem you want to solve or dream you want to pursue, someone, somewhere, has gone through a similar phase and overcome it. You can reach out to those people to find inspiration on what it takes to live a more creatively fulfilling life. Adam Grant, professor at the Wharton School of the University of Pennsylvania, says that getting in touch with important individuals is easy, as long as you: keep your message short, research the person beforehand, make your questions specific, and express gratitude.

YOUR CHALLENGE: Find someone who has accomplished a goal similar to one of yours, and reach out to him or her (by e-mail, snail mail, or even over the phone). Ask how they overcame challenges you face.

149. DOODLE BIG

The Canadian philosopher Marshall McLuhan once said: "The medium is the message." McLuhan was right: If you want to think creatively, you need to think big. And if the medium you choose isn't itself big, you're going to feel restricted both in what you're doing and your ability to think broadly. You can't, for example, envision much beyond the edges of a sheet of paper if your task is to draw within its edges. To think really big, you need to create really big, which means finding a big medium upon which to create.

YOUR CHALLENGE: Either find the biggest sheet of paper or canvas you can, and a really big paintbrush or marker, or get some sidewalk chalk and find an open area outside where you can doodle unrestricted. Doodle and draw to your heart's content in big and bold ways for at least 10 minutes.

150. CREATE YOUR OWN CHALLENGE

One purpose of this book is to help you see the world in new and exciting ways. By completing the challenges in this book, you should have ample motivation and inspiration for doing things a little differently and thinking a bit more creatively. What better way to demonstrate that than by coming up with your own creative challenges as a result?

YOUR CHALLENGE: Come up with a challenge of your own that helps you to see things in a new way. You can use any of the challenges in this book for inspiration, but you must come up with an original challenge of your own. Invite a friend to complete the challenge with you to consider this challenge completed.

"The thing about a clean sheet of paper is that it still has edges. . . . You can't do real work without edges, without something to leverage, but those edges don't have to be the same edges everyone else uses."

—SETH GODIN, AMERICAN AUTHOR, ENTREPRENEUR, AND PUBLIC SPEAKER

CATEGORY INDEX

SUBJECT INDEX

About the Author

TANNER CHRISTENSEN is a designer and creative strategist who started writing about the science and philosophy of creativity in 2008. Today he writes about creativity, ideas, and inspiration to an audience of hundreds of thousands on his website: CreativeSomething.net. He also writes, designs, and develops projects to help inspire and empower creatives around the world, including bestselling creativity apps, online courses, designs, and work for Adobe's 99U publication. Tanner currently resides in California, where he works full-time at Facebook. You can learn more about him and his work at tannerchristensen.com.